the

BREAK-
UP

YOU WILL BE OK!

workbook

Exercises & Advice to Help You
*Heal from Your Heartbreak &
Create Your Best Life!*

KENDRA ALLEN
@yourbreakupbestie

ADAMS MEDIA
NEW YORK   LONDON   TORONTO   SYDNEY   NEW DELHI

adamsmedia

Adams Media
An Imprint of Simon & Schuster, Inc.
100 Technology Center Drive
Stoughton, Massachusetts 02072

First Adams Media trade paperback edition September 2022

ADAMS MEDIA and colophon are trademarks of Simon & Schuster.

For information about special discounts for bulk purchases, please contact Simon & Schuster Special Sales at 1-866-506-1949 or business@simonandschuster.com.

The Simon & Schuster Speakers Bureau can bring authors to your live event. For more information or to book an event contact the Simon & Schuster Speakers Bureau at 1-866-248-3049 or visit our website at www.simonspeakers.com.

Interior design and hand lettering by Priscilla Yuen
Interior layout by Colleen Cunningham

Interior images © 123RF/cuppuccino, priatna, mikabesfamilnaya, samolevsky

Manufactured in the United States of America

1 2022

ISBN 978-1-5072-1917-1

CONTENTS

Part 4. Moving On in Your Journey 157

INTRODUCTION

So, you're going through a breakup.

Breakups are some of the most difficult experiences you will encounter in your lifetime—regardless of how long the relationship was or why the breakup happened. Every day can feel emotionally draining: You can't make it through the day without being reminded of your ex, social media is full of reminders of your relationship, you either can't sleep or you want to sleep all day, and deep crying sessions are the norm. Welcome to heartbreak....

While there isn't a magic pill that will shortcut getting over your ex (despite what the Internet might try to sell you), there is a way to heal from this heartbreak with dignity, grace, deep healing, and a more positive perspective about relationships moving forward. If this sounds appealing to you, you're in the right place. *The Breakup Workbook* will lay out a step-by-step process on how to move through this breakup with your head held high.

The best news I can tell you about the pain from a breakup is that it's going to pass. Though the journey of healing won't be linear, I can promise this deep hurt you feel in your chest right now isn't going to last forever. As you move through this process of getting over your ex, you may not always love the advice you hear. But the dozens of activities you will do over the course of this workbook will be an investment not only in your ability to let go of this relationship but also in your ability to turn this breakup into a blessing in disguise.

Over the course of this workbook, you'll learn how to:

* Reach out for help and utilize your support system
* Create a routine for optimal healing
* Detox from your ex
* Feel your feelings
* Let go of your anger and resentment
* Own your life single
* Move forward from this breakup
* And more!

Throughout this workbook, the focus is going to be on YOU! Not on what your ex is up to, how they're doing, or how they are healing. You're going to put all of your energy into *your* healing and transformation so you can start moving forward with peace and hope for the future. When things feel tough (which they very likely will from time to time), keep coming back to the reminder that this difficult time is going to pass.

Things *will* get better, you *will* heal from this breakup, you *will* be happy again, and you *will* find someone else to love again. Your healing journey starts now....

PART

1

ASSEMBLING YOUR FIRST AID KIT

Breakups are traumatic. Regardless of the circumstances that lead to your breakup, the fact that one day you have this partner in your life to share everything with and the next day they're gone and you're suddenly acting like strangers is extremely emotionally disruptive.

When you're going through heartbreak, it can feel like your entire life is ripped out from underneath you, yet you're still expected to go to work every day, pay your bills, and fulfill obligations to others in your life. It feels like you're barely able to keep your head above water.

In the first part of this book, Assembling Your First Aid Kit, we are going over how to do exactly that—you'll learn how to keep your head above water and maintain some semblance of a normal life so you can keep up with your day-to-day responsibilities. We are going to answer the question "Where do I even start after going through a breakup?"

Some people believe you need to immediately dive into the deep therapy work to get over your ex, others believe you should act like nothing happened, while others believe you should soothe yourself with pizza and ice cream. While there is no exact right way to navigate the beginning of a post-breakup period, the most important thing to be focusing on is releasing judgment of yourself. Give yourself the grace to deal with what you need to.

You'll notice throughout this first part of the book that the exercises focus on whatever gets you through your days. It's not about facing your triggers around your ex; it's not about forgiving your ex—we're just going to talk about taking it day by day, which is an approach you can use throughout your journey to heal from this heartbreak.

Breakups can often feel even more overwhelming than they already are when we look at long timelines. You're likely picturing this year's holidays without your ex, you're thinking about all the plans you made with them during your relationship that aren't going to happen, you're thinking about how your ex made promises you won't see come to fruition now. When you look at a breakup like that, it feels daunting. However, if you're able to look at just today and think, "How can I get through today?" your pain and heartache will feel much more manageable.

Over the course of the first part of the workbook, you'll notice a few themes pop out:

* Don't go through this alone.
* Distractions are healthy.
* Feel your feelings without judgment.
* You're not alone in how you're feeling.

Throughout this workbook, and particularly in this part, we're going to address a lot of myths and misconceptions people have around breakups. These myths can be harmful if they are preventing you from getting the help and healing that you need. For example, a common misconception is that distracting yourself from your feelings after going through something tough is counterproductive. Some people say that in order to heal from something, you must dive into the feelings headfirst and not run away from them. Is it important to feel feelings? Yes, of course. But sometimes the feelings after a breakup are too big, too powerful, and too overwhelming to be able to deal with so early in the process, and distractions can be really beneficial during that time.

Another coping strategy that has gotten a stigma is avoiding places you used to frequent with your ex. You're expected to "not let your ex prevent you from living your life," but in reality, someone who just went through a breakup typically isn't able to snap their fingers and let go of their ex entirely. In that case, it's a great and healthy idea to avoid as much as possible the triggers that will remind you of your ex.

The last misconception is that you need to uproot your life or do something drastic in order to get over your ex. It's a great idea to book some travel or even change your hair if you want to, but the best changes to make after a breakup are small daily changes. So much healing from heartbreak lies in the subtleties of your daily routine. We'll go through multiple exercises to create helpful morning and nighttime routines and a gratitude journaling practice.

One of the biggest issues I hear about from those going through breakups is how the mornings and nights are the hardest. There are not quite as many distractions available to you and you're spending a lot of time with your thoughts. Having consistent and planned morning and nighttime routines is key. In fact, preparation is key in general throughout your breakup.

It's a smart idea to plan what you'll do with your time when you have an open weekend coming up or a hard day on the horizon, or when the feelings hit out of nowhere. When you don't have a plan but have a lot of free time, I can guarantee you will spend most of that time reminiscing about your ex and the breakup. And if you don't have a plan for when big feelings suddenly hit, the phone is going to seem like it weighs a thousand pounds and it's going to feel too overwhelming to reach out to a friend for help.

You'll also see throughout this part that asking for help and surrounding yourself with a support system is a main theme. There is absolutely no reason to go through a breakup by yourself. We live in a connected world, and there are so many support systems out there. If you are someone who has a hard time asking for what you need, this is going to be great practice for you.

The final theme you'll see throughout this first set of exercises is all about non-judgment and avoiding shame. Breakups already cause enough pain on their own, and a mistake so many people make is to add shame and self-judgment on to that. Whether it's feeling shame that the relationship ended, judging the fact that your relationship "wasn't even that long," or feeling like you're the only person in the entire world feeling the way you do, none of it is worth the added pain you're giving yourself.

Every feeling you are experiencing is valid. At this very moment there are thousands and thousands of other people going through breakups, so you are far from the only person in the world experiencing what you're going through right now. You're going to have ugly thoughts entering your mind, saying, "You should be over this by now," but you need to keep coming back to the fact that your feelings are valid and they need to be felt so you can move past this heartbreak.

As you start implementing some of the tools in the following exercises, remember there is no magic pill for this breakup. The activities in this book won't take away your pain instantly, but if you practice them consistently, over time you'll begin to feel lighter and freer from this broken heart.

Let's Talk about It

Breakups need to be talked about. They are not something you can stash away in the attic and come back to twenty years later. The events, circumstances, feelings, progress, setbacks, and everything in between need to be discussed with other people.

A mistake many people make is believing that if they don't talk about their breakup, the pain will magically go away. If they act as if everything is fine, then maybe it will be. This just isn't true; the only thing that happens when you keep all your heartbreak to yourself is it magnifies and becomes worse.

Think of a time when you experienced anxiety or emotional pain and you didn't share it with anyone—you just let it rattle around and grow in your head until the problem became way bigger than it even needed to be. I'll bet that once you shared it with another person it instantly felt smaller and much more manageable.

That's what happens when you talk about your breakup—it takes some of the power out of it. A mentor of mine once said, "When you share your joy, you double it, and when you share your pain, you cut it in half," and that's incredibly helpful during something as tough as a breakup.

Talk Us Through Your Breakup

In the following exercise, you're going to have the space to write about your breakup. It's important to have an objective record about your breakup because, sometimes, the more you talk about it, the more the original story can get warped, and you end up falling into a certain narrative about what happened that may get further and further from the truth.

Use these pages to detail the events, overall circumstances, and biggest challenges of your breakup. If you're someone who is afraid to talk about the breakup aloud, this is a great way to get started, just getting the thoughts out of your head.

When did your breakup happen?

_____

_____

_____

_____

_____

How long was the relationship?

_____

_____

_____

_____

Were you blindsided by the breakup or was it expected?

_____

_____

_____

_____

Who ended the relationship?

_____

_____

_____

_____

Do you feel like you got closure?

_____

_____

_____

_____

What are you currently struggling with the most?

_____

_____

_____

_____

What Happened?

Write out the events and circumstances that led to your breakup.

_____

_____

_____

_____

_____

_____

_____

_____

_____

_____

_____

_____

_____

_____

_____

_____

_____

_____

_____

_____

_____

_____

_____

_____

_____

_____

_____

_____

_____

_____

_____

_____

_____

_____

_____

_____

_____

_____

_____

_____

Rally Your Support System

Breakups are not something to go through alone. They are too heavy of a weight to be carried by just one person, and it's unnecessary to face them by yourself. Let your support system help you!

Your support system can be friends, family, close coworkers, virtual friends—whoever you feel like you can rely on in your day-to-day life. These are the people who will help hold you up right now, when it feels like you can't hold yourself up, but there are two key components:

1. You need to ask for help first.
2. You need to ask for exactly what you need.

Many of us assume that our support system instinctively knows just how to support us. Well, the truth is, your support system will likely support you in the way *they* want to be supported—but that might not be helpful to you at all. The catch is that they'll never know this unless you say something.

You may have a friend who always wants to give advice when you really need someone to listen. You may have a friend who pushes you to go on a date when you're not ready. They likely mean well, but it's perfectly all right to ask them nicely to offer support in a way that works for you. This exercise will help you do that.

List Your Support System

Let's start off by taking inventory. In the left box, list the five most important people in your support system. In the right box, write why they are so important to you. For example: "Katie: a pillar in my support system because she's a great listener." "Tiffany: always up to plan an adventure to help take my mind off of what's going on."

How Do You Feel about Asking for Help?

It's time to think about whether you're open to support and to consider exactly what kind of support you need. Do you need someone to talk through your complicated feelings with? Do you just need someone to hug you and tell you it's going to be okay? Do you need tough love-style advice? Answer these questions to clarify your own feelings about support.

If you are someone who isn't used to asking for help or support, what is stopping you?

_____

_____

_____

_____

_____

Write what support would feel best to you right now.

_____

_____

_____

_____

_____

_____

Have You Rallied Your Support System?

One of the purposes of this workbook is to hold you accountable, so you will now answer true-or-false questions to see how you're doing with rallying your support system. If you answer "False" to any of these statements, don't be too hard on yourself—just move forward with sharing the news and getting the support you deserve.

The most important people in my life know about my breakup and what happened.

True   False

The most important people in my life know how I'm really doing, not just the facade I can put up.

True   False

I have made sure to ask the most important people in my life for help when I'm really struggling through this breakup.

True   False

I have shared with the most important people in my life how I'd truly like to feel supported by them.

True   False

Support System Well-Being Checklist

Often, what stops a person from leaning on their support system is that they fear they are being too much of a burden or their friends are getting sick of hearing about the breakup. Following is a checklist of things to make sure you're keeping in mind, so you consider others' well-being as you aim to improve your own.

☐ Make sure you're not putting all the pressure to listen on one person. Try to spread it out among others in your support system.

☐ Don't just dump all the negative onto them. Share with them what you're doing to heal, and make sure to share anything good going on in your life too.

☐ Even though you are the one in crisis, make sure you're asking others how they are doing as well.

☐ Remember, everyone you're talking to is an adult and can set a boundary with you if they need to.

Put Your Blinders On

After going through a breakup, almost everything probably reminds you of your ex. A song you hear on the radio, a car you pass on the road, or even certain foods can bring up memories. The world almost feels unsafe as you step back into it, because you're just waiting for something to set you off and remind you that you're going through heartbreak.

There are a lot of things you can't control throughout your day, like cars you pass on the road on your way to work. But there are also a lot of things you *can* control or at least put your blinders up to. A misconception is that being "strong" after a breakup means you need to face all your triggers head-on. You don't. That is your ego talking, and listening to your ego isn't what is going to help you get over your ex.

In fact, while your pain is fresh, it's a much better idea to block out any possible triggers so you can attempt to make it through the day without crying. There are enough reminders of your ex that you'll stumble on without any effort, so why not protect yourself in every way possible? At some point in the future, you'll be able to reclaim all these triggers and step out into the world without worry, but the beginning isn't the time.

Triggers to Avoid

In the following exercise, you'll identify some of the things that trigger you when it comes to your ex or your relationship. For the most part, these should be things you can avoid. For example, while you can't control the music that comes on at a restaurant, you can control the music you listen to in the car and what you're watching at home before bed.

List any TV shows or movies to avoid in the beginning of your breakup.

_____

_____

List music types or specific songs to avoid for the time being.

_____

_____

List places to avoid for now.

_____

_____

List any other things, events, or circumstances you should be steering clear of.

_____

_____

Safety Zone

Since the world can feel unsafe after going through a breakup, it is important that you take control and create a safety zone for yourself. This includes thinking of things you can watch or listen to and places you can go that are free of memories of your ex.

What are some breakup-safe TV shows or movies you *can* watch?
Think of anything that is funny or lighthearted where love isn't the main plotline. Avoid heavy love stories, and also avoid things that will raise your anxiety, like horror or true crime documentaries.

_____

_____

What are some breakup-safe things you can listen to?
This doesn't just have to be music, as music is innately more emotional. You can listen to funny or interesting podcasts or your favorite stand-up comedian while you're in the car. If you do choose music, listen to music you loved before your ex even came into the picture (think: music from your high school days).

_____

_____

Where are some breakup-safe places you can go with your friends?

These can be places you loved prior to ever meeting your ex, places you never went to with your ex, or (the best option) places you've always wanted to go to but never had the chance. Breakups are a great excuse to go to places and do things you've always wanted to. In keeping with the entry on how to ask for specific support, you can express to your friends that you'd like to go to or stick with these certain places.

_____

_____

Where are some places or who are some people you can visit that give you a feeling of safety and security?

This could be your parents' house or somewhere in nature.

_____

_____

Get Through the Day

In the beginning of your breakup, it's wise to just focus on getting through your days one at a time. Slowly but surely, you'll string days into weeks and weeks into months, and with time, you'll feel better. But the question becomes, "How exactly do you get through the days in the beginning?"

Many people report that morning and night are the hardest times after going through heartbreak. It makes sense—every morning you re-remember the breakup when you wake up, and nights are when you likely spent time with your ex. Plus, you don't have work or school as a distraction first thing in the morning and at night. So what do you do?

The key is building a routine that bookends your days in a positive way. The more predictably you can begin and end each day, the better your days will feel. Routines are so beneficial because not only do they help fill your time; they also empower you and help you feel more in control during a time when things may seem out of control.

Routines are also an investment in you. They are an act of self-love, and by doing a few things for yourself in the morning and at night, you're showing yourself and the world around you that you are worthy of caring and loving actions. In the following exercises, you will create a morning and a nighttime routine.

Which Activities Are Right for You?

If you're someone who has never had any type of self-care routine, don't worry—we're starting small. To begin brainstorming, check off any ideas from the following list that resonate with you, then add your own ideas at the end!

- ☐ Exercise.
- ☐ Take a bath.
- ☐ Meditate.
- ☐ Journal.
- ☐ Take a walk.
- ☐ Go outside.
- ☐ Read a book.
- ☐ Dance.
- ☐ Listen to uplifting music.
- ☐ Write affirmations.
- ☐ Make a gratitude list.
- ☐ Stretch.
- ☐ Call a friend.
- ☐ Send an appreciation text.
- ☐ Watch an uplifting video.
- ☐ Watch a funny video.
- ☐ Plan your day.

- ☐ Tidy up your space.
- ☐ Make your bed.
- ☐ Stay off your phone.
- ☐ Write a love letter to yourself.
- ☐ Take some quiet time.
- ☐ Light candles.
- ☐ Cook yourself something special.
- ☐ Make a cup of coffee or nighttime tea.
- ☐ Do a spiritual practice (e.g., prayer).
- ☐ Write down your fears and worries.
- ☐ Update your list of goals.
- ☐ Do an at-home spa treatment.

Plan Your Morning Routine

In this section, you'll outline an ideal morning routine. If you can't get to all of these every day, that is okay! Always try to do at least one, and make sure to select things that can be done in a relatively short amount of time so you can do them even in a rush. For example, instead of committing to 45 minutes of exercise, commit to 5–10 minutes of exercise.

Write down 3–5 things you can commit to doing in your morning routine.

_____

_____

_____

_____

_____

How many days per week can you commit to these?

_____

After doing this routine for three days, write down how it makes you feel to start your day this way.

_____

_____

_____

Plan Your Nighttime Routine

As you think about your nighttime routine, remember that you can also commit to things you will *not* do, like checking social media. You are likely going to feel a little extra vulnerable before going to sleep, so make sure this routine is nurturing and puts you in a peaceful and positive place before you try to fall asleep.

Write down 3–5 things you can commit to doing in your routine before going to sleep.

_____

_____

_____

_____

_____

How many days per week can you commit to these?

_____

After doing this routine for three days, write down how it makes you feel to end your day this way.

_____

_____

_____

Let's Practice Your Morning Routine

One of the best ways to start or end your day is by writing a gratitude list and repeating positive affirmations. Since break-ups can make your world look so dark, gratitude lists are a great way to help focus on the good things that still exist in your life. This list can include big things, like your health, or small things, like a really good cup of coffee.

Write down ten things you are grateful for.

1 _____

2 _____

3 _____

4 _____

5 _____

6 _____

7 _____

8 _____

9 _____

10 _____

Affirmations are short statements that can remind you that the pain you're experiencing is temporary and that someday something good will come out of this heartbreak. These should be "I" statements written in the present tense in order to help you visualize being healed.

Here are a few examples:

✳ I trust that this will pass.
✳ I accept my feelings as they are.
✳ I know one day this will be a blessing in disguise.
✳ I give myself permission to heal.
✳ I believe I will have a beautiful relationship someday.

Now try writing three affirmations of your own.

1 _____

2 _____

3 _____

Keep Busy

Distractions sometimes get a bad reputation because they can make it seem like you're simply sweeping feelings under the rug. But when you're going through the first couple of weeks or months after a breakup, when it feels like sitting with your feelings could drown you, distractions are a useful tool in your toolbox. Filling up your life as much as possible with plans, excitement, and socializing can help carry you through the beginning of your breakup recovery. These distractions can bring you to a time when you are emotionally ready to face those feelings.

In movies, people plan extravagant trips after breakups—which you could do, but it's not necessary. The key is to be around other people, doing things that will allow you to forget about the breakup for a while and get some relief.

The hardest times are when you're sitting at home alone with nothing to do and all the time in the world to THINK. (If you are sitting alone and thinking right after a breakup, I bet you're not thinking about anything positive.)

That's where making plans and getting busy comes in. If you look at your calendar, you should not see a lot of blank space. You don't want to burn yourself out, of course, but you should be making an effort to have at least a few plans every week.

Make Plans Happen

Plans don't happen out of thin air; they take some effort. Right after a breakup, they'll also take some accountability, since you're probably going to want to cancel each plan too. Your heartbreak wants you to isolate so it can thrive for longer. You can counteract that pressure to cancel by recording your plans here to emphasize that they're an important part of the healing process. These plans don't need to be fancy: Make a video-chat date with a friend, meet a coworker for coffee, or go for a walk with your sibling. Whatever you plan, write it down here and be sure someone else is involved.

1 _____

2 _____

3 _____

4 _____

5 _____

6 _____

7 _____

8 _____

9 _____

10 _____

Dealing with Weekends and Days Off

Even with all the planning you do, there is going to come a day when you have nothing on the calendar. You'll find yourself with just you, no plans, and infinite time to think about your breakup.

When faced with alone time on a day when you're feeling sad about the breakup, it's easy to fall into a paralysis where you end up on the couch all day. The good news is that you can also plan for days like this. Here's a sample list of activities you can do on those days. On the following pages, you'll assemble your tool kit of things you enjoy, so if you find yourself in sadness paralysis, you can revisit those pages and get into action.

Things I Can Do at Home

☐ Do a puzzle

☐ Garden

☐ Organize my closet

☐ Do an arts and crafts project

☐ Try a new recipe

☐ Have a home spa day

☐ Take a relaxing bubble bath

☐ _____

Things I Can Do for Free

☐ Take a bike ride

☐ Call a friend

☐ Go for a walk

☐ Read a book

☐ Volunteer

☐ People-watch

☐ _____

Things I Can Do to Treat Myself

☐ Book a massage

☐ Get a pedicure

☐ Go to the movies

☐ Go to a new restaurant

☐ Go shopping

☐ _____

Things I Can Do If I'm Feeling Adventurous

☐ Go for a hike

☐ Plan a trip with friends

☐ Take a mini road trip

☐ Try a sport or activity I've never done

☐ _____

Assemble Your Keeping-Busy Tool Kit

Now it's time to assemble your own tool kit that you can turn to on days when you have sadness paralysis and don't want to sit alone in your thoughts. You can use some of the ideas just offered and/or add your own.

Five things I can do at home:

1 _____

2 _____

3 _____

4 _____

5 _____

Five things I can do for free:

1 _____

2 _____

3 _____

4 _____

5 _____

Five things I can do if I want to treat myself:

1 _____

2 _____

3 _____

4 _____

5 _____

Five things I can do if I'm feeling adventurous:

1 _____

2 _____

3 _____

4 _____

5 _____

Planning Ahead

There will be certain days after your breakup that are harder than others, such as your birthday, your ex's birthday, your anniversary, and Valentine's Day. Think about days like this as you answer these questions.

Do you have any days coming up that you know will be tough?

_____

_____

_____

What can you proactively do to plan ahead? (For example, you can make plans or arrange a nice day for yourself.)

_____

_____

_____

Is there anything you loved to do but your ex didn't that you can do on that difficult day? (For example, maybe they didn't like a certain kind of movie that you like to watch.)

_____

_____

_____

Feel Your Feelings

No matter how many distractions you plan, you're still going to have feelings come up—and those feelings need to be felt. One of the key ways to truly heal from a breakup is by taking the time and space to feel your feelings.

Some people believe that if you just ignore your negative feelings, they will magically go away. That's just not true. If you don't take the time to acknowledge your feelings, they will get pushed down...but will eventually erupt at some point down the road. Not acknowledging your feelings can lead to long-term resentments, distrust in relationships, fear of dating again, and countless other issues.

So, what does "feeling your feelings" mean? Essentially, it means simply allowing yourself to recognize and sit with whatever feelings come up. If you start crying, you can recognize that it's perfectly normal and healthy to cry when something sad happens. The mistake many make is to judge their feelings. For example, if you feel happy, you may think it's okay—but if you feel sad, you might think you need to do everything in your power to make that feeling go away. Instead, tell yourself that there are no "good" or "bad" feelings; feelings just are.

Your feelings want to pass through you, and they will if you accept them as they are and have an outlet for them. However, if you judge your feelings and suppress them, they will stick around for longer.

How Comfortable Are You with Your Feelings?

In the following exercise, you are going to assess how comfortable you feel with your feelings. Having an awareness of your emotional coping skills is a great place to start in your healing journey. The purpose of this assessment is not to judge yourself—it will just give you an idea of where you might need a little work. Circle your answers to the following questions on a scale of 1–5.

How comfortable do you feel having strong emotions?

not comfortable   very comfortable

1   2   3   4   5

Do you believe that certain feelings are "bad" and should be avoided in any way possible?

strongly agree   strongly disagree

1   2   3   4   5

How confident do you feel in your ability to cope with your feelings?

not confident   very confident

1   2   3   4   5

How comfortable are you naming your feelings as they come up?

not comfortable   very comfortable

1   2   3   4   5

How can you better feel your feelings?

_____

_____

_____

_____

_____

_____

_____

_____

_____

_____

_____

_____

_____

_____

_____

_____

_____

_____

The Emotional Roller Coaster of a Breakup

As you'll learn when you go through the breakup recovery process, your emotions are going to feel like a constant roller coaster, and that is normal. You will feel a variety of feelings on any given day and potentially at any given hour. Just remember, this roller coaster won't last forever and it will get smoother and smoother as time goes on. The more you can familiarize yourself with your feelings and develop healthy ways to channel your feelings, the smoother the process will be.

First, familiarize yourself with your feelings. Check off every emotion you have felt within the last seven days. Again, it is very normal to fluctuate between many feelings every day.

☐ Sadness	☐ Denial
☐ Hopelessness	☐ Peace
☐ Powerlessness	☐ Confusion
☐ Shame	☐ Relief
☐ Anger	☐ Desperation
☐ Grief	☐ Acceptance
☐ Guilt	☐ Loneliness
☐ Shock	☐ Obsession
☐ Jealousy	☐ Fear
☐ Happiness	☐ Empowerment

Next, let's take a look at how you cope with these feelings. Check off which healthy tools you're comfortable using to channel your feelings.

☐ Crying

☐ Therapy or counseling

☐ Journaling

☐ Singing, drawing, or creative activities

☐ Talking to friends

☐ Exercising, dancing, or moving your body

☐ Writing letters

☐ Yelling

Freewriting

Now, you're going to practice writing exactly what is on your mind and allowing any feeling that wants to come up to surface and be recognized. Effective journaling is not about writing perfectly; it's just about forming a channel to process your emotions in a healthy way. If you catch yourself trying to explain your feelings or judging your feelings, pause just to notice that it happened, then continue writing. Set a timer for 5 minutes and try to write the entire time. Use extra paper if needed.

What You're Feeling Is Normal

In addition to overly judging your feelings, as we discussed in the last entry, another trap you can fall into is believing that your breakup is totally unique. You might think you are alone in what you are experiencing, that no one has ever had a similar experience, or that somehow the feelings and beliefs you have postbreakup are outside of the norm.

Everyone's breakup is unique in terms of the circumstances, but the feelings are universal. The danger of believing you are so unique is that you likely won't accept help from your support system because "they just don't get it," and you won't trust advice in general because you are so "different." Dropping these misguided beliefs will help you feel better faster.

The processing of emotions after a breakup is full of contradictions, and a lot of your feelings likely won't make sense. But just because something doesn't make sense, it doesn't mean it isn't valid or that it's not normal. People forget how traumatic and dysregulating a breakup is, and with that will come a lot of intense and opposing feelings.

Don't let the fear of being "abnormal" cause shame and prevent you from talking to your support system about the breakup. You heal by talking about it, and if you feel like you're the only person who's ever felt this way, you won't feel the freedom to process your feelings and you might also layer on shame.

Is This Normal?

The following exercise lists many statements about feelings after a breakup and asks you to answer whether you think they are true or false. You'll also write down why you selected each answer. This process will help you validate some of your experiences and feelings and explore any prejudices you have on how someone "should" feel while going through heartbreak.

It is normal to feel sad and mad at the same time when recovering from a breakup.

True   False

Why? What are your thoughts on this topic?

_____

_____

It is normal to miss your ex but not want them back.

True   False

Why? What are your thoughts on this topic?

_____

_____

It is normal to miss your ex and want them back even though they treated you really poorly.

True   False

Why? What are your thoughts on this topic?

_____

_____

It is normal to not be angry toward your ex even though you "should" and they've given you plenty of reasons to be mad.

True   False

Why? What are your thoughts on this topic?

_____

_____

It is normal to be sad and miss your ex even though you were the one who ended the relationship.

True   False

Why? What are your thoughts on this topic?

_____

_____

It is normal to still have hope your ex will come back even though it's clear the relationship is over.

True   False

Why? What are your thoughts on this topic?

_____

_____

It is normal to not feel like yourself and to feel completely out of control of your emotions and actions after a breakup.

True   False

Why? What are your thoughts on this topic?

_____

_____

It is normal to second-guess yourself and only think about the "could have"s and "should have"s that might have been different.

True   False

Why? What are your thoughts on this topic?

_____

_____

It is normal to not want to talk about the breakup and to defend your ex just in case they come back.

True   False

Why? What are your thoughts on this topic?

_____

_____

    The answer to every single one of these questions is true. These are all extremely common and normal experiences and feelings to have after your heart gets broken. Do they all make perfect sense? Absolutely not, but again, it's important to validate these feelings instead of fighting against them. These feelings are all temporary and they will pass with time as you work through the healing process.

How Can You Accept Your Feelings More Freely?

Being able to accept your feelings as they are is an important part of the healing process. Accepting sadness, anger, depression, and grief now will actually allow you to feel better in the long run. The sooner you can accept your feelings, even if they don't feel good, the sooner they will pass.

Do you have any other thoughts, feelings, experiences, or circumstances from your breakup that you believe to be "abnormal"? Why do you think they aren't normal?

_____

_____

_____

_____

_____

How can you be more kind and validating toward yourself?

_____

_____

_____

_____

_____

PART 1

ASSEMBLING YOUR FIRST AID KIT *Review*

After completing the exercises in Part 1, you should feel more equipped to handle your day-to-day life while going through your heartbreak. The goal is to add more tools to your coping toolbox and get you more comfortable utilizing these coping skills so you can keep your head above water.

Remember, you are still at the beginning of your healing process. You're able to cope with your feelings better, but that doesn't mean the feelings aren't strong. Breakups are an emotional roller coaster, though as you move through the rest of this workbook, your broken heart will feel more and more put back together.

In this part, we covered the importance of talking about your breakup, leaning on your support system, putting blinders on to avoid triggers, getting into some healthy routines, filling up your calendar with plans, feeling your feelings, and more.

Let's Recap

Use these questions to recap this part before moving on to the next one.

✦

In this part, you learned the importance of a support system. You should not be facing heartbreak by yourself. It's crucial to be honest with those you love and trust and allow them to support you in your healing. You also learned the importance of asking for exactly how you need to be supported.

Have you been surprised at how your support system has shown up for you after you asked?

_____

_____

_____

_____

_____

_____

✦

You learned about creating routines, putting blinders on, staying busy, and making plans to help positively distract you in the beginning, right after a breakup. Distractions can often get a bad reputation, but they are crucial when your feelings are so large and so intense during heartbreak.

As you've begun to implement these tools, what has been the most effective thing to help you cope?

_____

_____

_____

_____

_____

_____

✦

We discussed the importance of feeling and accepting your feelings. There is no wrong way to feel after a breakup, and no matter how you're feeling, you are not alone. Breakups come with intense feelings that don't always make sense, and they don't have to make sense to be valid. The more you can accept your emotions, the faster you'll be able to work through them.

After learning all of this, how have you approached your feelings in a more accepting way?

_____

_____

_____

_____

_____

_____

DETOXING FROM YOUR EX

Going through a breakup is really dysregulating; in other words, it turns your world upside down. You talk to someone every single day—possibly even living with them, sharing just about everything—then a breakup happens, and suddenly your whole life changes.

You are no longer in a relationship with that person, but you still have constant daily reminders of them. You have old romantic text messages on your phone, you have photos of them around your home, you're wearing a gift they got you.... In the beginning, it feels impossible to escape the reminders and memories of your ex. Their departure is so sudden it can feel like a death, and you're left picking up the pieces of your life without them.

There are so many habits and reflexes you've developed as part of your relationship that aren't talked about as part of the breakup recovery. When you wake up in the morning, either you expect to roll over and see your partner or they're the first person you text. Then you go to work, and something happens with your boss. Your partner was probably the first person you would text and vent to or ask for advice. When you're at work, you're thinking about your dinner plans or what you're doing after work, and that was something you always discussed with your partner. Your weekend plans, travel plans, anything on your mind would all have been discussed with this person, and they are not there for that.

It is a habit to pick up the phone and text them. It is a habit to call them on your way home from work. It is a habit when you see that meme to send it over to them. These habits may seem like "not a big deal," but they are a huge aspect of the healing process. This person is completely intertwined with almost every aspect of your life, so there is a lot of habit breaking and unlearning to do so you can get to a place of peace without having them around.

The Detoxing from Your Ex part of this workbook is all about how to take the steps needed to start clearing your ex from your life and breaking those habits. For example, you'll learn you can start clearing your environment of reminders of your ex so you can reach a sense of peace in your day-to-day life.

This detoxing process is necessary whether your relationship was "good" or "bad." Many people believe that getting rid of reminders around your place, cleaning up your social media, and ridding your phone of photos is only something you do if you have hatred toward your ex. That's not necessarily true. Detoxing doesn't mean you need to go violently destroy your ex's stuff, and it isn't something you do AT your ex. Rather, it's something you do as a way to protect your heart as you're moving on.

Another part of the dysregulation you can experience is a feeling of emptiness. It might feel like an intense craving or a deep yearning to talk to your ex, see your ex, or even send them a text. There is a reason for this deep pit you're feeling in your stomach. When you're in a relationship with someone you're in love with, your body and brain are pumping you full of feel-good chemicals like oxytocin, serotonin, and dopamine. When the source of those feel-good chemicals is gone, your body goes into a kind of withdrawal. This is why people say a broken heart can feel physically painful.

While your body is going through this physical withdrawal, it's even more important that you're doing whatever you can to make your environment as supportive as possible. If you're continuing to see your ex or look at old photos, it will make the process longer and more difficult. And if you keep photos of your ex readily available on your phone or still follow them on social media, it makes the temptation to reach out much greater.

When we get to the Detox from Your Ex Checklist, you'll see a list of things to remove in and around your space. You can instead add to your home uplifting messages, more pictures of loved ones, and/or photos of places you want to visit.

As you go through the exercises in this part, you may find yourself asking, "Is this detox really necessary? Can't I get over a breakup without going fully No Contact? Do I have to stop looking at my ex's social media?" And to be honest, you can get over a breakup without doing all those things; it's always possible to get over a breakup.

But do you know what else is possible? It's possible to get from California to New York by bicycle. It's possible to dig a trench using a spoon. Are those the fastest options? Absolutely not. Are they efficient? Also no. Will they cause unnecessary pain and frustration? Yes.

That's exactly what happens when you take the approach of not detoxing from your ex. If you try to stay friends, still frequent their social media, and keep reminders of them all over the place, you are making the breakup much harder on yourself, and it will very likely take longer for you to get over them. You deserve peace and happiness as quickly as possible.

As you go through this next group of exercises, you probably won't feel good about it right away. In fact, you may notice that you feel worse in the short term when you go No

Contact and get rid of your ex's stuff. The good news: That's completely normal. All of these exercises are meant for the long-term healing from your breakup—they aren't quick fixes (remember, there are no quick fixes after breakups). You need to think of them as a long-term investment in you and your ability to heal your broken heart.

It's also completely normal to unfollow your ex on social media only to go back and try to look at their page a few hours later. Just because you go through these exercises doesn't mean you are going to be "perfect" through this detox or that you won't have temptations. Breakups are meant to be taken a day at a time. You may have a really hard day when you are keeping tabs on your ex's social media and have to fight every cell in your body not to call them, and that's okay! Tomorrow is going to be a new day. As you go through this next part, you will be getting all the practical tools you need to jump-start this healing process.

A note for those of you who are in a coparenting relationship with your ex: If you share children, you obviously cannot cut your ex out of your life completely. There still needs to be civil contact for the sake of your children, but there are still plenty of ways for you to heal. As you go through this part, use the exercises as inspiration for how you can create your own version of the No Contact Rule. You're allowed to still have boundaries in place with your ex, and if you can dictate certain guidelines, your heart is also protected.

Deal with Logistics

Breakups are incredibly emotional by nature, but amid the intense feelings, there are likely some logistics that need to be worked through. These feel more like business and can seem out of sync with the emotional storm you're currently experiencing.

Even though facing some of these logistics can feel like pouring salt in your wound, it's important to take care of them sooner rather than later. Anything that's keeping you connected with your ex is going to make your healing process drag out longer than it needs to.

Some of the most common logistics involve canceling trips or plans, swapping stuff, handling a mutual friend group, and deciding whether to stay friends. In the following exercises, you will learn how to navigate each of these. (You will notice there's a theme of limiting contact with your ex as much as possible.)

Even though you'd probably love an excuse to see your ex, most of the time it isn't necessary. Whenever you see your ex, it's going to cause an emotional disturbance, old feelings will come back, chemicals will rush in, and you'll have to face the fact that you're broken up all over again. If you proceed in dealing with these logistics with a mindset of moving on, you're more likely to achieve a sense of emotional peace around the breakup.

Tying Up Loose Ends

Often when a relationship ends, there are things like planned vacations, money that's owed, or upcoming plans or events to sort out. Although it feels like the last thing you want to deal with, it's important to tie up these loose ends to decrease your anxiety and free up your energy to pour into your healing.

Are there any loose ends you need to tie up with your ex? Make a list of any situations you need to attend to.

_____

_____

_____

_____

_____

What is your plan to deal with those loose ends? This could involve direct communication with your ex, or you could ask a mutual friend to help deal with it for you.

_____

_____

_____

_____

_____

The Stuff: How to Return and Swap It

After you've spent a significant amount of time with someone, it's likely you have their clothing or other miscellaneous items of theirs around your place. Many make the mistake of turning a swap into an emotional reunion, or anytime they find something of their ex's, they'll treat it as an excuse to reach out and see them. None of this is necessary.

The goal is to limit (and hopefully get down to zero) interactions between you and your ex so you have the space to breathe, let go, and heal. Returning things is not an excuse to disturb your emotional peace. Instead of reaching out and seeing them, you have a few options such as the ideas listed here.

What is your plan for swapping stuff?

- [ ] **Have a friend handle it:** Your friends want to help support you, and this is something they can easily handle without the emotional attachment you have.
- [ ] **Drop off without contact:** If your ex has a porch, leaving a box there is another great option.
- [ ] **Mail it:** Returning stuff doesn't need to require a face-to-face interaction or even communication, for that matter. It can be as simple as going to the post office and mailing everything back. Obviously, this will cost some money.
- [ ] **Meet up:** This wouldn't be a first choice, and if you decide on this option, make sure you're aware of the emotional repercussions that could come from that interaction.

Whatever you do, get the stuff returned as soon as possible.

How to Navigate Mutual Friendships

During a relationship, it's natural to combine social circles and have a group of friends you share, but it is still possible to get the space you need to heal after the relationship ends. An important thing to remember is that it's not necessary for your friends to pick sides—they can opt to stay close with whomever they choose. But it's up to you to set the boundaries you need to let yourself heal and enjoy social events.

Keep in mind that you're allowed to choose which social events you attend. For example, if there's a big birthday party coming up that your ex will attend, you can reach out to the birthday person and ask to take them out separately.

Are there events coming up that you and your ex are both invited to? If so, what are your plans to handle those events?

_____

_____

_____

Friends should not be expected to choose sides. However, it is important that your friends know how you feel. Are there any conversations you need to have with mutual friends?

_____

_____

_____

Can You Be Friends with Your Ex?

Let's talk about why being friends with an ex is a bad idea....

It's because your heart doesn't have an off switch. You can't tell your heart, "Hey, you know that person we've been in love with? Now you need to just see them as a friend. We can't have any more romantic feelings for them, and if they want to date other people, we can't get mad, because they're just our friend now." That's a very difficult change to accept. Not only that, but every time you see them or talk to them your old feelings for them are going to arise and it's going to feel like a major setback in your breakup healing.

Even if you told your ex you agreed to be friends, you're allowed to tell them later that it's not going to work right now. The most important thing at the moment is to attend to your own feelings. Pretending you're okay being friends with your ex often means you're not attending to your feelings—you're ignoring them.

Do you believe you can be friends with your ex? Why or why not?

_____

_____

_____

_____

_____

_____

If you think you can be friends with your ex or are on the fence, here are some questions you can ask yourself.

Would you be okay with inconsistent (meaning not daily) communication?

Yes   No

Would you be okay if they told you about someone new they were seeing?

Yes   No

Do you honestly think you could move on and date other people if you stayed friends?

Yes   No

Are you just staying friends only to be friends and not because you want to get back together?

Yes   No

If you answered "No" to any of these questions, it is likely that you're not ready for a friendship with your ex and that pursuing a friendship will do far more harm than good to your healing.

Obey the No Contact Rule

The No Contact Rule is as simple as it sounds: After a breakup, you cut all contact with your ex. No texts, calls, social media messages, or seeing each other. What isn't as simple is the intention behind it. Some naysayers will insist it's a way to get back at your ex, but the sole purpose of the No Contact Rule is to help you get over your ex faster and more easily.

The point of a breakup is to be able to learn how to live happily without your ex, so if you're staying in consistent contact with your ex, you're missing the point. Breakups require space, and they require you to turn to people other than your ex for support and companionship.

Even though the rule is simple to understand, it's not necessarily easy to follow. You must see it as the equivalent of ripping off a Band-Aid so the pain stops faster. The reason No Contact is so important is because every time you even see your ex's name pop up on your phone, you're going to feel an emotional reaction. Every time you talk to your ex, it's not going to match your expectations or what you wanted them to say. It's dragging out your pain, and it's reinforcing the heartbreak.

Consider Your Thoughts on the No Contact Rule

There are a lot of misconceptions out there about No Contact and what the purpose of it is. Some of the biggest misconceptions I hear about it are that it's meant to hurt your ex and that it will somehow ruin any chance you have at getting back with your ex. Neither is true. The No Contact Rule is solely to protect you and get you the space you need to heal your broken heart. Even after reading that, you might have your own thoughts about the rule. Answer the following questions to see where you stand.

After learning about the No Contact Rule, how do you feel about following it?

_____

_____

What is your honest intention in following the No Contact Rule?

_____

_____

What are your fears surrounding No Contact?

_____

_____

What to Do Instead of Contacting

There will come a time when you feel tempted to reach out to your ex. It's important to have a plan for what to do instead of giving in to the temptation. Having some enjoyable activities in mind that take 30 minutes will help you fill the time till the desire passes. After you compile this list, take a picture of it and keep it on your phone so you're always prepared. When you feel tempted to reach out to your ex, what will you do instead? Here are some examples to get you started:

☐ Write out what you want to say to your ex in a journal instead.

☐ Text a friend and ask how their day is going.

☐ Go for a walk without your phone.

☐ Watch some funny videos on *YouTube* or *TikTok*.

☐ Take a shower or bath.

Use the following lines to make your own list of fun things you will do instead of reaching out to your ex.

_____

_____

_____

_____

_____

The No Contact Contract

No Contact isn't easy, but this agreement and commitment to yourself will serve as a reminder of your end goal to heal and get over your ex. In this contract, you will write what you're committing to, why you're making this commitment, who you've shared this with (for accountability), and what you'll do when an urge to reach out to your ex hits.

This is something else you can take a photo of and keep on your phone for the times when you feel vulnerable to reaching out.

MY NO CONTACT CONTRACT

I commit to:

I'm committing to this because:

I have shared this contract with ————————————— .

When I feel like contacting my ex,
instead I will:

Signed: ——————————————————————————————

If You Slip and Backtrack

Sometimes the temptation gets too big and you end up calling or texting your ex. Take a deep breath—it's okay. It's normal to slip up. Just don't let one lapse make you lose all the progress you've made. First off, stop the conversation. Let them know that it was a mistake and you need to go back to not having contact with them. The next time you're tempted to reach out, read through this worksheet to help decide whether it's worth doing it again.

How did you feel before you reached out?

_____

_____

How did you feel right after and in the following days?

_____

_____

Did their response meet your expectation?

_____

_____

If you could say something to the version of you right before you reached out, what would you say?

_____

_____

How to Deal with Social Media

Twenty years ago, no one had access to their ex's actions and whereabouts quite like they do today thanks to social media.

Nowadays, social media provides infinite opportunities to see what your ex is up to—who they are hanging out with, how they're doing, and even how often they're going to the gym or what they're eating. With all this access, recovering from a breakup can become much harder, because your ex is still present in your life via social media.

Most people are probably aware that looking at their exes' social media doesn't make them feel good, yet they continue to check out their profiles for weeks and months after break-ups. Why? The answer varies: You may be wanting to maintain a sense of control, you might be attempting to preserve your ego and not appear hurt, or you may be trying to remain "top of mind" for your ex. Or it might be that *not* knowing what they're up to is too much, and it drives you to obsessively look.

You are likely on social media multiple times a day, so the temptation to look can be high. Luckily there are some things you can do to lessen the temptation and put some obstacles in your way to keep you from impulsively looking every time you open an app. The following exercises will help.

Cleanse Your Social Media of Your Ex

When it comes to removing your ex from your social media, there are three options:

1. Mute your ex on all social media.
2. Remove them as a friend or unfollow them.
3. Block them.

The third option is going to be the best in terms of protecting your heart, though it may take some time to feel comfortable blocking them. But if you start by muting your ex, you may still find yourself looking at their profile every single day, which obviously isn't helpful to your healing process.

"But isn't blocking so harsh and immature?" you ask. Remember, it's far more harsh and far more immature to ignore your feelings and continue a connection on social media despite how much it triggers your heartbreak.

You are allowed to mute, unfriend, unfollow, or block anyone on social media if they are disturbing your emotional well-being and your sense of peace. This applies to your ex's friends and family and honestly anyone who makes you feel worse about your situation.

Use the following table to determine and track which of the three options you will be using on each of your social media platforms.

	Mute	Remove as friend or unfollow	Block
Facebook			
Instagram			
Twitter			
TikTok			
Venmo			
Other: _____			

Manage Your Profile

When it comes to photos of your ex on your social media profiles, what you do is up to you. If you find yourself repeatedly scrolling through past photos, it's probably time to take them down. Some social media sites have a great feature called "Archive" that will simply hide the photos from your feed if you don't want to delete them altogether.

Sometimes an unspoken competition arises between exes to see who removes photos and changes their relationship status on social media first. If your ex removes the photos first, you'll probably think that they're being cruel or harsh, or that you never meant anything to them. However, if your ex leaves your photos up, it's going to cause confusion and mixed messages on whether they still want you back. It's a lose-lose scenario.

Another scenario that arises is the "But what if I want my ex to see how well I'm doing?" question. That is a normal thought to have, but by doing this, you're not getting back at your ex, you're actually just wasting energy on them. Every time you go to post something, you're thinking about how your ex is going to react to it, and that's putting your energy in the past, not the future. This exercise gives you room to think about what your social media plan will be.

What are you planning to do with the photos of you and your ex on your social media pages? Circle one.

Leave up   Delete   Archive

Why did you make that choice?

_____

_____

_____

_____

_____

_____

_____

Now that you've gone ahead and made a decision, how do you feel?

_____

_____

_____

_____

_____

_____

_____

Making Peace with Other Profiles on Your Feed

You can mute, unfriend, unfollow, or block anyone on social media who doesn't positively contribute to your emotional well-being and sense of peace at the moment. For example, if you have a friend who just got engaged and won't stop posting sappy photos, you might want to mute them for a little while.

Is there anyone you need to mute, unfriend, or unfollow who is making your breakup pain feel worse?

_____

_____

_____

_____

Set a timer for 5 minutes and scroll through your feeds, muting, unfriending, or unfollowing anyone who disturbs your emotional peace.

How do you feel after doing that?

_____

_____

_____

_____

Developing a Healthy Relationship with Social Media

Social media can be an incredibly helpful tool after a breakup if you allow it to be. It's all up to you and how you set up your feed. If you keep your ex on there, you're likely going to feel anxious about what you might see. But you could use social media to stay in touch with friends, follow positive mental health accounts, or learn about events in your area. This exercise will help you think about how you can use social media to make yourself feel better.

What are some additional boundaries you can set around social media? For example, setting time limits for certain apps, etc.

_____

_____

_____

_____

How can you use social media as a positive place for you?

_____

_____

_____

_____

Actively Detox from Your Ex

Now that we've covered how important it is to let go of your ex and heal from this breakup, it comes down to action. When your life is so intertwined with someone else's, it helps to have a clear list of steps you can take to detangle those attachments.

This is where the Detox from Your Ex Checklist comes in. It's a list of action items that will help reduce the number of times you're triggered to think about your ex during the day. Clearing memories from your home and phone will ensure you are not surrounded by reminders all day.

There's always a draw toward looking at old memories when you're feeling sad about your breakup. On a rough day, you'll feel tempted to go through your old text threads or look at photos, which will only make you feel worse. This is why it's crucial to take these action steps in the beginning to clear out your space. This process can help you protect your heart as you heal.

Detox from Your Ex Checklist

There will likely be items on this list that you don't want to do yet, and that's normal. It may take some time and some trial and error before you can see the true value of removing these things from your life. To make the process easier, have a good friend walk through this with you so you have built-in accountability and support.

To begin, scan through the whole list and pick one thing that feels the easiest to start with so you can begin with a win and build some confidence and momentum.

What will be your first commitment?

_____

_____

_____

☐ **Delete the text thread conversation you have with your ex on your phone.** It's very easy to scroll up in your conversation so you can relive the sweet and happy messages you exchanged with them.

How do you feel after deleting the conversation?

_____

_____

_____

☐ **Change your ex's name in your phone.** If you've used a pet name, some heart-eye emojis, or any other endearing descriptions in your ex's contact in your phone, strip them out. You can change their contact to just their formal name or delete it entirely. You'll also want to remove them from your "Favorites" list. When you're trying not to contact your ex, the fewer reminders you have of them when you open your phone, the better.

How do you feel after changing their name?

_____

_____

_____

☐ **Clear away the mementos and photos you have around your home that are connected to your ex.** You don't need to throw them all away or burn them Taylor Swift–style by any means, BUT it's important that they are out of sight, out of mind as you're healing your heart. I would suggest putting everything in a box and either stashing the box away somewhere (like in your garage) or giving the box to a friend to keep for the time being.

How do you feel after clearing your place?

_____

_____

_____

☐ **Remove relationship photos and videos from your phone.** This is the number one way I see people emotionally torturing themselves after a breakup: They take constant trips down memory lane by looking at old photos and videos. You don't need to delete all the photos, but transfer them off of your phone so they're less readily available. (You can utilize services like Google Photos or Dropbox to store the photos in case you want them after you're healed.)

How do you feel after removing the photos?

_____

_____

_____

☐ **Disconnect from any accounts you share with them (e.g., Amazon, Netflix, HBO).** You don't need to see what they are watching or what they are buying postbreakup. It's far too easy to make up a story or assign meaning to every TV show or movie they watch. I can also assure you that any money you need to spend to have your own accounts is well worth your peace of mind and ability to heal.

How do you feel after disconnecting from their account?

_____

_____

_____

☐ **Change your phone background.** If you had a picture of you and your ex as a phone background, of course you're going to want to change that to avoid the constant triggering. However, even if you didn't have a photo of you and your ex there, it's a great opportunity for another fresh start. Try picking a positive quote as a background for an encouraging reminder.

How do you feel after changing your background?

_____

_____

_____

☐ **Delete playlists you had with your ex.** Music is highly connected to relationships, so it's likely that you made at least one playlist in your music app that was all of you and your ex's songs. Again, this may be something you turn to when you're feeling down that will only make you feel worse.

How do you feel after deleting those playlists?

_____

_____

_____

☐ **Ask your friends to not share any news they get about your ex with you.** It's very tempting to want to hear gossip or updates about how your ex is doing, but there is no piece of news that will make you feel better. Your friends likely won't realize that sharing information could be harmful, so it's much easier to set the boundary with them in the beginning to avoid issues later on.

How do you feel after sharing this request with your friends?

_____

_____

_____

Is there anything else you think you're missing in your detoxing process? Be sure to be honest with yourself now to prevent any unnecessary triggers later on.

_____

_____

_____

A week after completing this checklist, come back and write down any changes you've felt since clearing these things out.

_____

_____

_____

Stop Playing Investigator

After going through a breakup, many people fall into the habit of wanting to play "investigator" on their ex. This involves looking at the ex's social media and asking friends what is going on with them, and it can even be taken to the point of driving by your ex's house or workplace (not recommended). The reason playing investigator is so tempting is because it gives you a false sense of control.

Breakups take away so much of your control, and so it is natural to want to grasp onto any amount of control you can find. Some people report that keeping tabs on their ex gives them something to focus on other than the fact that their relationship is over.

Playing investigator on your ex creates a connection to your ex, which is why for some it may feel positive in the moment. But in reality, it's hurtful, because you're trying to *break* that bond between you and your ex in order to heal from your breakup.

What Kind of Investigator Are You?

One of the first steps toward stopping your investigating is to become aware of how you are doing it. Before jumping into the true-or-false questions, remember, these are all incredibly common behaviors, and there is nothing to feel ashamed of if you are doing any of these. As you go through these statements, reflect back on what you wrote in the Detox from Your Ex Checklist and think about how doing each of these has made you feel.

I have checked my ex's social media profiles.

True   False

I have looked at my ex's friends' and family's social media trying to get information.

True   False

I have looked at my ex's transactions on *Venmo*.

True   False

I have looked at my ex's Netflix or other streaming service to see what they are watching.

True   False

I have asked friends how my ex is doing.

True   False

I have asked my friends to check dating apps to see if my ex is on there.

True   False

Recognizing the Lose-Lose Game

Why is it so detrimental to play investigator on your ex? Because no matter what information you uncover, it will not make you feel better. If you find out your ex is happy, going out, and/or traveling, it will make you feel awful. If you find out your ex is really struggling, that will also make you feel awful. It's essentially a lose-lose game.

Has finding out information about your ex ever made you actually feel better about yourself?

_____

_____

_____

Has finding this information ever helped you feel better about the breakup?

_____

_____

_____

How do you usually feel after "investigating"?

_____

_____

_____

A Letter to Your Future Self

Even with all the knowledge that it's not helpful, there will be times when you're tempted to investigate what your ex is doing. Sometimes your past self may be the only thing that can prevent you from doing it again, so write that future version of yourself a letter encouraging you to rethink that choice. Let your future self know how crummy it can feel to get updates about your ex or backtrack in your healing every time you get new information about them. This is a great exercise to practice right after doing something like looking at your ex's social media, when you might have regrets, so those feelings are still fresh.

Dear future self,

If you're tempted to check out your ex's profiles on social media or otherwise, read this first....

_____

_____

_____

_____

_____

_____

_____

_____

In Case of Emergency

You can turn to this exercise when you know you shouldn't be looking into your ex's life but are really tempted to do so anyway. This exercise will offer you ways to stop yourself, like calling a friend or rereading your journal pages. Journaling may help you get in touch with your emotions just enough to remind you that you don't want to hurt yourself even more.

Following is a checklist of things you can do to help stop yourself from investigating your ex.

☐ Check in with a friend.

☐ Read your future-self letter.

☐ Do some journaling (see prompt on this page).

☐ Leave your phone inside and go for a walk around the block.

☐ Put on a funny TV show to watch until the distraction passes.

☐ Write a list of things you're thankful for right now.

☐ Take a long shower or bath.

Why do you want to look at your ex's life at this moment? Are there any particular feelings that are motivating you? How do you think you'll feel afterward?

Stay in Your Own Lane

When a relationship ends, you and your ex are on separate roads, in two separate lanes, and for you to heal most effectively, it should stay that way. This means that figuring out what your ex is up to, what they're thinking, how they're feeling, who they are hanging out with, what they thought about the breakup, what they think about you, and so on is none of your business. The more you make it your business, the more frustrated you will become and the more likely it is that you'll make negative and unnecessary assumptions about yourself (for example, thinking, "I meant nothing to them").

Making these sorts of negative judgments about yourself and your relationship will not help you heal. If you didn't get perfect closure, you might feel the need to keep reaching out to your ex until you get your answers...but that only extends your pain as well.

Instead, focus on your own healing by doing the exercises in this book and looking ahead to your future. The activities in this section will help you keep your attention on yourself and your path.

Are You in Your Own Lane?

A person will go to great lengths to get the answers they want from their ex, and usually with no success. Typically, all this does is keep you stuck in your heartbreak longer than you need to be. The more you are trying to get answers or information from your ex's lane, the less time you're spending on healing, which is where all your energy should be going. This exercise is a chance to take inventory and find out in what ways you have been out of your lane.

Are there any unanswered questions you have about your breakup? These might include not having closure and wondering how your ex feels about the breakup, why they ended the relationship, and/or how they're dealing with the breakup.

_____

_____

_____

_____

_____

_____

_____

_____

_____

_____

What have you done to get answers to these questions from your ex?

_____

_____

_____

_____

_____

_____

_____

What do you feel like you'll achieve if you learn these answers? (This question is important, because most of the time you will not achieve what you think you will.)

_____

_____

_____

_____

_____

_____

_____

_____

Let Go of How Your Ex Is Moving On

Envisioning your ex partying without you, taking a vacation without you, and dating someone else can be torture. But do not fall into the trap of thinking that anything your ex does postbreakup somehow invalidates the relationship they had with you or makes you any less of an important person. Your ex is simply moving on in the best way they know how to, just like you are. Answer the following questions to assess how well you are doing at letting go of your ex.

Do you feel concerned about how your ex is moving on?

_____

Do you feel like how your ex is moving on is a reflection of you and your relationship? Why or why not?

_____

_____

_____

_____

_____

_____

How much time each day do you spend thinking about what your ex is doing, thinking, and/or feeling?

_____

How to Stay in Your Lane

Now that it's clear why you should stay in your own lane, the question is HOW. How can you stop the obsessive thinking about your ex and what they are thinking, doing, and/or feeling about you and the breakup? The single best thing you can do is to *focus on yourself*. The more you focus on how you are feeling, what you're thinking about, and what you need for support, the less you're going to obsess about your ex's lane. The following questions will help guide you toward investing your healing energy into yourself.

What does staying in your lane mean to you?

_____

_____

_____

_____

_____

_____

_____

_____

_____

When you get hyperfocused on what your ex is thinking, doing, and/or feeling, how can you focus on yourself instead? (Ideas: Ask yourself how you are doing, talk about how you're feeling with a friend, journal, buy yourself flowers, go for a walk, do a meditation.)

_____

_____

_____

_____

_____

_____

_____

Remember, how your ex is healing from the breakup is not a reflection of you, your worth, or your relationship. You are the only person who can determine your worth. What are your thoughts on this statement?

_____

_____

_____

_____

_____

_____

Affirmations to Help You Stay in Your Lane

The reason it's so tempting to find out how your ex is handling the breakup is because the unknown can be incredibly unsettling and can make you fill in the blanks with the worst-case scenario. Affirmations are a powerful way to remind yourself that even though you may not know all the reasons and information right now, it's okay—you'll still be able to heal from this breakup without knowing all the answers. The following are some affirmations to try repeating to yourself. Read through them first, create your own on the blank lines (or feel free to edit these suggestions), then read them out loud every day for the next fourteen days and watch how it changes your mindset.

✳ I don't have all the answers, but I will move on anyway.

✳ I trust that how my ex is moving on has nothing to do with me.

✳ I have the power to care for my emotions, and I don't want to give my energy to my ex's feelings.

✳ I am the only person who can determine my worth.

_____

_____

_____

_____

_____

_____

Set Some Boundaries

Even if you remove reminders of your ex from your space and focus on your own healing, other people can intentionally or unintentionally disturb all your hard work.

Maybe you made the tough decision to go No Contact with your ex, only to have them continue to reach out to pester you into being friends. Or your well-intentioned family members may tell you they never thought it was going to work with your ex anyway. Your friends may push you into dating far sooner than you're ready because they don't like seeing their friend in pain.

Setting boundaries can help you manage each of these tricky situations. There are many definitions of boundaries, but in this case, "boundaries" refers to how you teach other people to treat you. It's you telling others how they can speak to you, what kind of support you need, what is okay to say, and what is not okay to say. When you are going through something like a breakup, it's extremely important that you protect yourself and your energy, and boundaries can help you do that.

My favorite motto surrounding boundaries is "Say what you mean, mean what you say, but don't say it mean." There is a misconception that boundaries are rude or mean; they aren't. They simply set a standard for how you'd like to be treated.

Prepare to Set Some Boundaries

During this next exercise, we're going to go over some of the most common boundaries you may need to set with your ex, your friends, and your family. If there is a boundary you feel like you need to set or may need to set in the future, check the box and write out your own script for how to discuss it. I've given you some ideas on how you can frame the conversation, but make sure you're writing something that feels authentic to you.

Boundaries for Your Ex

☐ If your ex keeps reaching out:

"Please stop contacting me. I've asked you nicely to stop reaching out so I'm able to get the space I need to heal, and I'd appreciate if you could respect that wish of mine. If you don't stop, I'll have to block you."

Now write your own script here.

_____

_____

_____

_____

☐ If your ex keeps pushing you to be friends:

"I know we agreed to be friends in the beginning, but it isn't working for me anymore. I'm not able to heal from this breakup and be friends with you at the same time, so I'd appreciate if you could respect my wishes and stop asking me about it."

Now write your own script here.

_____

_____

_____

_____

☐ If your ex's friends or family members are reaching out and it's making you feel worse:

"I appreciate you touching base with me, but at the moment it's too hard for me to have contact with you as I'm healing from this breakup. If anything changes in the future, I will reach out and let you know."

Now write your own script here.

_____

_____

_____

_____

Boundaries with Your Family

☐ If they talk about how much they liked your ex:

"This isn't really helpful, and it's actually making me feel worse since I already miss them. I would appreciate if you could refrain from saying that while I'm around."

Now write your own script here.

_____

_____

_____

_____

☐ If they are asking how you are doing too much and it becomes overwhelming:

"I appreciate that you are concerned about me and want to make sure I'm okay. I'm still in the middle of processing everything, but I'll let you know if I need anything or any support."

Now write your own script here.

_____

_____

_____

_____

☐ If they say they never thought it would work anyway:

"I know you're trying to be helpful, but this really isn't helping, and it's actually making me feel worse. Can you please not say that to me?"

Now write your own script here.

_____

_____

_____

_____

Boundaries with Friends

☐ If they are trying to tell you news about your ex:

"I'm working on trying to heal and let go, and as much as I want to know news about my ex, it's not helping my healing process. If you hear stuff about them in the future, I'd appreciate if you didn't share it with me."

Now write your own script here.

_____

_____

_____

_____

☐ If they are trying to trash-talk your ex, but you're not comfortable doing that:

"I understand why you think this would be helpful, but it's not. I'm not in a position where I can talk negatively about them, and it just makes me feel worse. Can we talk about something else?"

Now write your own script here.

_____

_____

_____

_____

☐ If they are trying to pressure you into dating:

"I love that you're trying to get me back out there, but I'm still hurting and focusing on my healing. I think if I tried to date right now, it would actually hurt more."

Now write your own script here.

_____

_____

_____

_____

Fears Around Boundaries

Some of these conversations may seem difficult to engage in, but remember, you are well within your rights to set the boundaries you need to. Think of your heart after a breakup as a construction project. Construction projects need fences and structures to protect them while they are in progress, and your energy and emotions may need the same thing. Use the following questions to work out any fears you have around setting these boundaries and to consider any more boundaries you may need to set that weren't included in the previous exercise.

How do you feel about needing to set these boundaries?

_____

_____

_____

_____

Are there any additional boundaries you need to set with your friends, family, or ex?

_____

_____

_____

_____

PART 2
DETOXING FROM YOUR EX Review

Separating your life from your ex's can be one of the toughest parts of going through a breakup. It makes the breakup feel more final, more real, and therefore more painful. The way to view this detoxing work is as a long-term investment. I'm sure you experienced uncertainty, fear, and pain removing your ex's photos from your phone or taking them off your social media, but it is something you will be so grateful you did six months down the road.

Before moving on to the second half of the workbook, let's review and recap Detoxing from Your Ex.

Let's Recap

Use these questions to recap this part before moving on to the next one.

✦

In this part, we busted a lot of myths and focused on why it's important to detox from your ex as much as possible. What some might see as avoidance or immature cutting off has now been established as a necessary step in the healing process.

After going through this part, how has your perception of detoxing from your ex changed?

_____

_____

_____

✦

It can be extremely difficult cutting a significant figure out of your life, and even though you know it will help in the future, it can be painful in the present.

What has been the hardest part for you going through Detoxing from Your Ex?

_____

_____

_____

✦

As you move through the rest of the healing process, things will come up that you wish you could say to your ex. That's a natural part of the journey, and it's completely normal.

Before moving on to the second half of the workbook, is there anything you wish you could say to your ex?

_____

_____

_____

✦

The point of detoxing from your ex is so that you are able to focus solely on you and your own healing. The more you concern yourself with what your ex is up to, how your ex is feeling, or how they're doing after the breakup, the less energy you're investing in yourself.

After going through the detox, do you feel more inspired and better equipped to focus on yourself?

_____

_____

_____

PART 3

HEALING AND REBUILDING

Healing from a breakup is a process. It's like an onion—you've got to peel away multiple layers before you can get to the core of it. You've likely experienced a lot of different layers of your breakup already. You've had angry days, peaceful days, sad days, and depressed days, and you may be wondering when you're going to be able to exit this emotional roller coaster you've been on. The good news is that even though you still probably have really hard days, of course, you have also likely had glimpses where you're starting to feel better. That's what we want to build on.

In the early stage following your breakup, your feelings and emotions surrounding the breakup were too big and too overwhelming to process right away. You may have felt too overwhelmed by sadness to even get up for work, so it wouldn't have been a good idea to dive deep into processing that sadness. The anger you felt probably made it hard to see straight, so you wouldn't have been able to process that anger in a calm way. Now that you've had some healing and some distance from the initial heartbreak, though, it's time to start addressing those feelings more directly.

This is what I like to call "processing." You may have heard this term on social media before, but what does it mean? When you go through something emotionally painful, your body doesn't like the feeling of pain, so it will shove the pain as far away as possible as quickly as possible. This is a great feature in the short term, but in the long run it can cause suppressed emotions and emotional distress. On the other hand, processing feelings means identifying and validating the emotions you're feeling, allowing yourself to experience the feelings without judgment, and then, if necessary, taking action to help you feel better.

When you don't take the time to process your feelings, it can leave you still feeling angry at your ex years down the road. You don't want to hold on to that negative energy for all that time. Not processing your feelings can also cause you to feel distrust in your future relationships and can cause you to make unwise partner choices down the road.

So, how are you going to process your feelings? The first step is to assess where you are in the breakup. What feelings are still coming up for you when you think about your ex and the breakup? Have you been able to accept that the breakup happened, or are you still holding on to the hope that you and your ex are going to get back together? Are you blaming yourself for the breakup? Is your self-esteem suffering because of the breakup? Are you feeling empty because you don't have your partner anymore?

The answers to these questions are going to determine where you still need some healing. It's common to struggle with anger, denial, sadness, poor self-esteem, and despair, but it's also necessary to put in the work to heal each of those areas. You want to be able to walk away from the breakup feeling empowered, fulfilled, excited about the future, and positive.

This next part is divided into two sections: healing and rebuilding. The healing section is going to address the leftover wounds you are still feeling about the breakup. Right after the breakup happens, your whole existence feels like a wound, everything triggers you, and it's hard to find any amount of time when you don't feel heartbroken. Now that the dust is beginning to settle from the breakup, you can start looking at when you are still feeling those deep wounds.

From there, those wounds can be in one of two buckets: They can be things you're feeling toward your ex—anger that they left, anger that they cheated, anger that they didn't fight for the relationship, and so on. They can also be wounds that you are feeling toward yourself, which are very common but not often addressed. These self-directed wounds include resentments you're feeling toward yourself for something you believe you did wrong within the relationship or potentially being mad at yourself for being in a relationship with your ex in the first place.

Another self-directed wound may include your self-esteem. No matter how confident a person you were before the breakup, heartbreak will almost always impact your self-esteem negatively. We will spend a full section going over how to rebuild your self-esteem.

When examining the pain and loss you're still experiencing, you may find yourself feeling discouraged. It's a lot easier to get over the initial pain of a breakup and then try to move on like nothing ever happened without digging deep. But that's not how you achieve long-term peace and completely move on from your ex. Doing this work isn't always fun, but it is critical for your well-being and perspective on relationships moving forward.

The second half of this part is all about rebuilding and filling the void left by the breakup. Now that you have that distance from the initial breakup, we'll be looking at when you're still missing things from your relationship, along with how to refrain from judging yourself harshly for having these feelings. We'll come up with a plan to fill the void in a healthy way so you can move on with your life feeling full and satisfied.

Another part of rebuilding has to do with your identity. It is common to tie too much of your identity to your partner when you are in a relationship, and if that relationship ends, you wind up feeling unsure of who you are anymore. We will explore how to rediscover your identity outside of the relationship that just ended and talk about the importance of having an identity outside of relationships in general.

The work you'll do in this part will make you much less likely to jump right into a new relationship to make these icky feelings go away. There's nothing wrong with dating (we'll get into moving on in Part 4), but it's just too easy to try to use a new partner to erase the void and open wounds left by your ex. To heal those wounds, you need to do some self-reflecting, not dating. By processing your feelings, being your own advocate, and feeling whole and complete on your own, you are setting yourself up for a lifetime of healthier relationships.

By healing, you're taking the steps to get over your ex, and by rebuilding, you're giving yourself the freedom to always feel okay whether you're in a relationship or not. Obviously, there's nothing wrong with wanting to be in a relationship, but in a society that sells you on finding "your missing piece" or "your other half," it can feel difficult to feel happy when you're not in a relationship.

So, as you go through these exercises, don't be afraid to peel back the layers of your emotions. Remember this: The ultimate goal isn't just to let go of your ex; it's to give yourself the freedom, motivation, and confidence to move forward.

Accepting the Breakup

It's not easy to accept a painful situation. However, to move through this breakup, it is essential that you come to a place of acceptance.

One of the biggest blocks to getting over a breakup is not accepting the reality of the situation, and that's because there are a lot of misconceptions about what it does and doesn't mean to accept the heartbreak:

* Accepting doesn't mean that you must approve of the situation. You can be mad at the situation and still accept it.
* You can disagree with the reason for your breakup and still accept that it happened. You're still allowed to feel like the reason is wrong, unfounded, or too flimsy.
* Accepting doesn't mean that you're not standing up for yourself. It means you're making the conscious decision to accept the situation for your own benefit, so you don't have to fight anymore.
* Accepting doesn't mean that you're letting anyone "get away with" something. You can accept that your ex sees the relationship differently than you and that's their right. It doesn't mean you have to like it or approve of their behavior.

If you fight the breakup, all you're doing is running in circles instead of moving forward. Fighting with reality is a lose-lose game. Accepting is for YOU, not for your ex. It's to give you the opportunity to let go and move on instead of causing yourself stress by fighting with reality.

What Are You Struggling to Accept?

It's completely normal to not want to accept a breakup at first; it takes time to get there. Let's start by taking a look at what part of your breakup you're having trouble accepting. For example, maybe you're not accepting how your ex ended the relationship, the reason for the breakup, or your ex's behavior since the breakup. Answering the following questions will help you identify where you need help accepting what happened.

What parts of your breakup are hard to accept?

_____

_____

How has not accepting the situation negatively affected you and your ability to heal?

_____

_____

Many people don't want to accept situations because they are afraid of what it means if they do. For example, if you accept the breakup, you will ruin your chances of getting back together with your ex. What fears do you have around accepting the breakup?

_____

_____

_____

How to Accept the Breakup

Once you've identified the areas you need some help with, the question becomes, "How do you actually accept a painful situation?" One technique is to "act as if"—in other words, act like you have already accepted it and then behave with that mindset. Actions can change thoughts. Taking action day by day can change your perspective. These questions will help you imagine what you'd do if you *did* accept the breakup.

If you accepted the breakup, you wouldn't be reaching out to your ex, begging for them to come back. What would you be doing instead?

_____

_____

_____

_____

_____

_____

_____

_____

_____

_____

If you accepted the breakup, you wouldn't be waiting around for your ex to change their mind. What would you be doing instead?

_____

_____

_____

_____

_____

If you accepted the breakup, you wouldn't be constantly keeping tabs on your ex's social media. What would you be doing instead?

_____

_____

_____

_____

_____

In what other ways could you act as if you accepted the breakup?

_____

_____

_____

_____

_____

Visualize Your Acceptance

Sometimes accepting something can be seen as giving up, surrendering, or losing. This couldn't be further from the truth. Acceptance is actually very empowering and can bring a huge amount of inner peace. However, because it's easy to get so stuck on the illusion that acceptance is giving up, you forget about the benefits. In this exercise, you are going to focus on what it will FEEL like when you accept that the breakup happened. When you reach that point, will your anxiety have gone away? Will you feel lighter? Will your chest not be so tight? Will you be able to see a future without your ex? Close your eyes and visualize yourself in a place of acceptance, then write how it feels.

Describe how you would feel if you accepted the breakup.

_____

_____

_____

_____

_____

_____

_____

_____

_____

Letting Go of False Hope

When recovering from a breakup, it is natural to cling to a sense of hope. It could be hope that your ex is going to change their mind and ask for you back, hope that your ex is going to change their behavior, or hope that your ex will become able to commit to your relationship. You've likely heard all your life that it's a good thing to be hopeful and optimistic—but in the case of breakups, hanging on to hope can keep you anchored to the relationship much longer than is necessary.

The dangerous part of hanging on to false hope is how that hope might affect your actions. It's okay to secretly think about how you want your ex to come back, but it's harmful to your healing if you decide not to move on just in case they change their mind. False hope will pass as long as you don't act on it. Remember, it's normal to fantasize about the relationship coming back together, so do not judge yourself for having those thoughts.

Perhaps the most convincing reason to let go of that false hope is the knowledge that if you're meant to end up with your ex, you will. But it won't happen by waiting around or hanging on to something your ex said during the breakup that could be interpreted as encouraging. It'll happen in the natural course of you moving on with your life.

Has Your Ex Given You False Hope?

During the actual breakup, your ex may have said things that gave you hope of getting back together. Your ex may have felt badly about breaking up with you and then inadvertently said things that sounded encouraging to you, such as "Who knows what the future will hold?" or "Someday maybe we can work it out." Whether or not your ex was genuine in saying those things, again, it's important not to act on anything other than a clear "I want to get back together" statement.

Your ex may also be sending mixed messages by reaching out to you, asking to get together, or giving you other requests that contradict the fact that you're broken up. If your ex wants to get back together, they won't communicate with you in code. A random "hello" text from your ex doesn't mean you should drop your healing and prepare to go back to them. In the space here, you'll think about whether you've interpreted any communication from your ex as a sign that you might get back together, creating false hope.

Has your ex said or done anything that has given you a false sense of hope?

_____

_____

_____

_____

_____

Your Honest Hopes

It's common to want to get back together even though you can recognize the relationship wasn't right. It's also common to have been the one to end the relationship yet still hope your ex will change and it will work out. This topic may not be something you're comfortable discussing with loved ones, because you may be ashamed about it or it just may not make sense to others why you want to be back with your ex.

Even though it might not make sense to anyone else, it's important not to judge yourself or feel shame around your hopeful thoughts. The following questions will help you write about any hopes you're harboring at the moment.

What kind of hope are you hanging on to when it comes to your relationship and your ex?

_____

_____

_____

_____

How do you feel about the fact that you have this hope?

_____

_____

_____

_____

Time to Release

Surrendering the hope of you and your ex getting back together isn't something that can happen all at once. The thoughts are going to keep returning periodically, and that's okay—just keep releasing them and focus on moving forward, not backward.

In the spaces provided, write a thought you're releasing and what you hope for instead. Here are some examples:

✳ I release the thought that my ex and I will get back together, and I trust that the right partner for me will come along.
✳ I release the thought that I can fix my ex, and I trust that it's not my job to fix them anyway.

Anytime you find yourself obsessing on false hope, come back to these statements to reread them.

I release ————————————————————————————,

and I trust ————————————————————————————.

I release ————————————————————————————,

and I trust ————————————————————————————.

I release ————————————————————————————,

and I trust ————————————————————————————.

I release ————————————————————————————,

and I trust ————————————————————————————.

The "Could Have"s and "Should Have"s

With a breakup come the inevitable "could have"s and "should have"s. The "could have"s and "should have"s are the thoughts you have when you meticulously go back through your relationship and try to figure out how you could have done things differently to prevent the breakup.

If your relationship was meant to be, nothing you could have said or done would have messed that up. If your relationship was NOT meant to be, you could have done everything "perfectly" and it still would have ended. Take that pressure off yourself. The way to get over a breakup is by loving yourself, not shaming yourself.

Were you perfect in the relationship? No—not a single person on the planet is perfect in their relationship. Do you have some lessons to learn and some growing to do from this past relationship? Yes—the point of life is that we get to keep learning and growing. But there's a big difference between lying awake at night running through every conversation and interaction you've had with your ex and beating yourself up about it, and being gentle with yourself and allowing yourself to learn as you go through the healing process.

Just like no good will come out of looking at your ex's social media, no good will come out of obsessing on these "could have"s, and no good will come out of beating yourself up for something you believe you did to cause the breakup.

Treat Yourself Like Your Best Friend

Typically, you are your own harshest critic (by far!), and this is especially true when you get into the "could have"s and "should have"s. When you are feeling low, you are not seeing the situation clearly, and it's likely you have completely lost perspective.

The best way to get out of that mindset is to take a step back and pretend you are talking to your best friend. For example, let's say you're being too hard on yourself for being too needy in the relationship, and in your mind, that caused the breakup. If your friend came to you and said they thought their neediness caused a breakup, what would you say to them?

You wouldn't say, "Yep. You are so needy, and that totally ruined your relationship." You would say something like, "You're an awesome catch for someone. You're being way too hard on yourself. You deserve someone who can meet your needs."

In this exercise, you'll write out the things you're being too hard on yourself about. After each of those things, write what you would say to your best friend instead. This will help you be nicer to yourself and should help guide your internal conversation to a more positive and compassionate place.

What are you being too hard on yourself about?

What would you say to your best friend if they told you they were beating themselves up about the same situation?

_____

_____

What are you being too hard on yourself about?

_____

_____

What would you say to your best friend if they told you they were beating themselves up about the same situation?

_____

_____

What are you being too hard on yourself about?

_____

_____

What would you say to your best friend if they told you they were beating themselves up about the same situation?

_____

_____

Be Kinder to Yourself

After a breakup, you need to practice a lot of self-compassion and kindness toward yourself. However, it can be really difficult to do that, so it takes some effort.

Write yourself a pep talk to pull you out of the times you're obsessing on the "could have"s and "should have"s.

_____

_____

_____

_____

_____

What are some practical ways you can be kinder and more compassionate toward yourself?
For example, starting each day by repeating a couple of affirmations either in the mirror or in your journal, or writing down two things you're proud of at the end of each day.

_____

_____

_____

_____

_____

Get Mad

Anger is an emotion that unfortunately can be seen as negative or unproductive. The reality is that it's normal to feel angry after a breakup, whether it's anger about how your ex broke up with you, how your ex treated you in the relationship, or how your ex is treating you after the breakup. Those are all circumstances that could make you mad. Anger is actually a vital emotion to experience when recovering from a breakup.

If anger isn't dealt with in a healthy way, it tends to come out sideways—you might send an angry text to your ex or flip out on a friend who has nothing to do with the breakup. There is no reason to judge yourself for being mad, nor is there any reason to keep it inside, where it will do far more damage.

So, how do you deal with anger in a healthy way? The key is to express the anger in a way that is productive. For example, you might write about your anger in a journal, vent about it to an understanding friend, or even take a kickboxing class and picture the punching bag as your ex. These suggestions will help get that angry energy out of you and will bring another layer of healing to your heart.

Dear Ex, I'm Mad

One really effective way to express your anger is by writing a letter to your ex. The most important part of writing this letter is remembering that you will *never* send it or read it to your ex. This exercise is for YOU, not your ex. In this letter, you will write all the reasons you're mad at your ex. This letter can include everything from slight annoyances to full-blown rage. Think of it as a way to clear your head for more positive thoughts.

If you want to, you can read your letter to a friend so you can process what you wrote. It's normal to feel emotionally activated after writing this, but you'll notice in the days following that you will feel lighter.

Dear ex,

_____

_____

_____

_____

_____

_____

_____

_____

_____

How Does Anger Feel?

You may find yourself angry at people or things that you aren't *really* mad at. For example, maybe it's a friend who just got engaged. This is also normal, and it's okay to feel that way even if they don't deserve it. Just recognize that it's probably misplaced anger at your ex. The following questions will help you determine how you feel about anger in general.

How do you usually express anger?

_____

_____

How does it feel when you express anger?

_____

_____

Do you feel guilty when you get angry? If so, why do you suppose that's true?

_____

_____

Is there anyone else besides your ex who you're angry at? Who, and why?

_____

_____

Release Any Anger You Have at Yourself

It's normal to feel mad at yourself after a breakup. Unfortunately, many people ignore the anger they direct toward themselves. Whether it's for not seeing the red flags, making some kind of mistake, staying in the relationship longer than you should have, or settling for less than you deserve, there are many reasons you may be upset at yourself.

It is vital to clear away the anger you have so you can move on with a sense of peace. In the space here, write down any lingering anger you're feeling toward yourself.

Dear self,

_____

_____

_____

_____

_____

_____

_____

_____

_____

_____

Rebuilding Your Self-Esteem

Breakups can take a major toll on your self-esteem. They can make you feel less than worthy and as though you are not enough and can make you question how you feel about yourself. A breakup itself is enough to make you feel awful and in pain, but if you add to it feeling poorly about your character, your appearance, or any other parts of you that your mind is attacking, it can make the breakup feel unbearable.

Whether your ex said something that explicitly hurt your self-esteem (insulting you, putting you down) or you're feeling low because they broke up with you, rebuilding your self-esteem is so important when you're healing from heartbreak. Self-esteem will obviously help you feel good about yourself, and it will also help you in future relationships. Having low self-worth puts you at risk for getting into a relationship that's less than you deserve.

If you are someone who has relied on partners and your relationship status to give you self-esteem in the past, this is an incredible opportunity for you to learn how to feel good about yourself as a single person. There is nothing more powerful than knowing and owning your worth.

So, how do you actually rebuild your self-esteem? In the following exercises, you will learn practical approaches to doing that. For now, know that it all comes down to seeing yourself objectively and then taking action through what I call "esteem-able acts."

How Is Your Self Esteem?

Self-esteem may be something you have struggled with since middle school, or this breakup may have caused a new crisis in confidence. It's important to determine *where* you get your sense of self-worth from. If you're someone who has always relied on other people for your self-esteem, it's likely this breakup had a bigger impact on you.

Before this breakup, how was your self-esteem?

_____

_____

Are you someone who has relied on other people for your self-esteem? If so, how do you do that?

_____

_____

What impact did this relationship have on your self-esteem?

_____

_____

How did this breakup affect your self-esteem?

_____

_____

What Do Others Love about You?

It's difficult to see yourself objectively, especially after a breakup. You're your own harshest critic, and the voice in your head is probably not being very nice to you. If someone were to ask what you like about yourself, you may have a hard time answering that right now. In this exercise, you will ask your loved ones to think of things they like about you to bolster your self-esteem and outlook.

Ask three people close to you for ten things they love about you. They can be qualities you have, things they respect or admire, or just reasons why they love you. (It may feel awkward to ask, but I bet they'll be happy to do it.)

_____

_____

_____

_____

_____

_____

_____

_____

_____

_____

What Do You Love about You?

After getting a pep talk from your loved ones, now it's your turn to write what you love about yourself. Your list can include qualities, physical attributes, talents, character traits, anything you'd like. You can repeat the things your friends said about you, but make sure you dig deep to write new ideas too. Twenty-five items may seem like a lot, but quantity is important—do not move on until you have used all the lines.

Write down twenty-five things you love about yourself.

_____   _____

_____   _____

_____   _____

_____   _____

_____   _____

_____   _____

_____   _____

_____   _____

_____   _____

_____   _____

_____   _____

_____   _____

_____

Build Self-Esteem with Esteem-able Acts

Self-esteem isn't something you just wake up with one day—it comes from doing many things, big and small, that make you feel good about yourself. I call these "esteem-able acts." To help think of esteem-able acts, ask yourself, "What would make me feel good about myself today?"

Check off the esteem-able acts you want to start incorporating into your life. Add your own ideas at the end.

☐ Exercise.

☐ Volunteer.

☐ Practice a random act of kindness.

☐ Call a friend, ask how they're doing, and be a good listener.

☐ Practice validating my own feelings.

☐ Rest if I'm tired.

☐ Set boundaries when I need to.

☐ Keep a gratitude list.

☐ _____

☐ _____

☐ _____

☐ _____

☐ _____

Filling the Void Left by the Relationship

When you lose a romantic partner, you're going to be left with a void. That void is the source of a lot of the pain you're feeling from the breakup, and it can manifest itself in a lot of different ways. It can make you feel empty and lonely, like you've lost a sense of yourself, and maybe even like you've lost your identity.

This void is caused by a combination of things. You miss:

* Your actual partner and their characteristics, like how they could make you laugh
* How you felt as a person within the relationship
* How your ex made you feel
* The things you and your ex used to do together
* Just being in a relationship in general

When you look at all these things, it's no wonder you're hurting! The mistake many people make following a breakup is that they don't do anything to fill that void. When the void is left open, it can lead you to fill it with unhealthy coping skills or fast-track you into a rebound relationship.

Even though you're no longer with your ex, it doesn't mean you've lost all the ways to find joy and fulfillment in your life. The following exercises will help you assess your void and think of uplifting, positive ways to fill it.

Let's Look Into the Void

The first step in filling the void is going to be taking a look at what you are missing because of this breakup. These can be things you miss about your ex, things you're missing about yourself from the relationship, things you're missing about the relationship itself, and so on. Write down whatever comes to mind—nothing is too small. Even things like missing a certain meal your ex used to make can impact your life.

When you think about the loss of your relationship, what things are you missing?

_____

_____

_____

_____

_____

_____

_____

_____

_____

_____

_____

_____

Let's Find a Substitute

Now that you're aware of all the things you're missing, it's time to find some alternative ways to fill the void. In the space here, list each of the things you're missing from the previous exercise and then write one or two ideas of how you can substitute. Here are some examples:

I miss our Friday date nights.
Instead, I can plan to go out with my friends on Friday nights when I would be really missing my ex.

I miss having someone to talk to when I'm struggling at work.
Instead, I can reach out to my friends or family members when I need advice about work.

I miss the way my ex used to always compliment me.
Instead, I'm going to write compliments to myself on sticky notes and put them on my bathroom mirror.

I miss ⎯⎯⎯⎯⎯⎯⎯⎯⎯⎯⎯⎯⎯⎯⎯⎯⎯⎯⎯⎯ .

Instead, ⎯⎯⎯⎯⎯⎯⎯⎯⎯⎯⎯⎯⎯⎯⎯⎯⎯⎯⎯⎯⎯

⎯⎯⎯⎯⎯⎯⎯⎯⎯⎯⎯⎯⎯⎯⎯⎯⎯⎯⎯⎯⎯⎯⎯ .

I miss ⎯⎯⎯⎯⎯⎯⎯⎯⎯⎯⎯⎯⎯⎯⎯⎯⎯⎯⎯⎯ .

Instead, ⎯⎯⎯⎯⎯⎯⎯⎯⎯⎯⎯⎯⎯⎯⎯⎯⎯⎯⎯⎯⎯

⎯⎯⎯⎯⎯⎯⎯⎯⎯⎯⎯⎯⎯⎯⎯⎯⎯⎯⎯⎯⎯⎯⎯ .

Missing Your Ex versus Missing a Relationship

Another reason breakups can feel more painful than they need to be is because your ex and relationships in general become intertwined. In your mind, the things you're missing and feel like you've lost translate into the idea that you'll never find someone who makes you feel like that again.

Sure, there are certain things you'll miss about your ex specifically—but don't forget, a lot of the pain you're feeling stems from just missing being in a relationship. And remember, you will be in another relationship again.

In the space here, write what you miss about your ex and what you miss about just being in a relationship.

_____

_____

_____

_____

_____

_____

_____

_____

_____

_____

Regaining Your Identity

When you're in a relationship, your identity can get intertwined with your partner's and can also be defined by the fact that you're in a relationship. Part of the healing process requires that you redefine who you are as a single person.

Many people neglect their individual identities while in relationships. Especially during the beginning stages, you may neglect certain hobbies that are important to you or neglect friends because you want to spend all your time with your new partner.

Adjusting to being on your own can seem daunting, but try looking at it as an exciting opportunity. The beauty of being on your own is that you can choose to be whoever and do whatever you'd like. Breakups are an ideal time to explore new hobbies, try a new fashion style, change your hair, take a trip, change jobs, and so on. Breakups can give you the courage to do things you normally wouldn't, so take advantage of that—it's a reason why people make big changes during heartbreak.

While you don't want to make big changes to run away from the pain, it's okay to make changes because you're feeling empowered, free, or motivated. If you take an empowered stance and get to know yourself in a new way, you'll find adjusting to being single can be a beautiful thing.

What Have You Neglected?

Relationships are fulfilling, but they can take away the time you need to focus on yourself. The things you were doing to feel good before you met your ex—like spending time with friends, self-care, personal development, and hobbies—may have been dropped when you first started dating. Now is a great time to add those things back into your life.

What parts of you did you neglect during the relationship?

_____

_____

_____

_____

_____

How do you plan on reincorporating those things into your life?

_____

_____

_____

_____

_____

_____

Defining Your Identity

Many of us choose to define ourselves by who we are as partners in romantic relationships or by our relationship status. But there are so many amazing things about you that have nothing to do with being in a relationship! Thinking about those things now will help you remember what makes you *you*.

Take time to journal on how you define yourself. Don't mention anything about relationships or what kind of partner you are.

_____

_____

_____

_____

_____

_____

_____

_____

_____

_____

_____

_____

_____

Single Bucket List

Breakups can give you a sense of courage you may not normally have to do things like travel, change jobs, or move. Doing things that are out of your comfort zone will not only build your self-esteem, but also make you feel like a strong and capable individual.

Write down twenty things you have been wanting to do—big or small. These can include a restaurant you want to try in your local area or a big trip you've always wanted to take. Make it a goal to cross off as many things as possible in the coming months.

_____   _____

_____   _____

_____   _____

_____   _____

_____   _____

_____   _____

_____   _____

_____   _____

_____   _____

_____   _____

Reclaiming

Most of a breakup is about leaving things behind, and it's easy to forget that each relationship shapes you moving forward. You were with your ex for a reason, and there were things you did as a couple—hobbies you picked up, favorite weekend activities, favorite shows you used to watch together—that you might want to continue doing. Just because you two are no longer together doesn't mean you need to abandon all those things.

Reclaiming places, activities, and hobbies for yourself as you move forward is a powerful way to move on from a breakup. For example, if your ex introduced you to hiking during your relationship, go hiking with a friend to reclaim it. Some things may take some time to reclaim, but your ex doesn't "own" any of those things.

What are some things from your relationship that you want to reclaim for yourself moving forward?

_____

_____

_____

_____

_____

_____

Overcoming Setbacks

Healing is not a linear process. Getting over a breakup is going to be an emotional roller coaster, where you could be feeling like you're making great progress and then a week, a day, or even an hour later you're feeling in complete despair. This is all normal. Even if you follow all the guidelines, do all the work on yourself, and invest in your healing, you are still going to have days that are really hard. Setbacks are just part of the healing process.

Think of your breakup as a video game with different levels. As you move through the process, you're going to master one level and then go up a level. When you level up, it's going to feel a lot harder again, and you're going to have painful feelings come up. So when you do have an emotional setback, instead of thinking that you're moving backward, think of it as leveling up—which means you're that much closer to being over your ex.

Setbacks can also be triggered by things like reaching out to your ex or looking at their social media. But remember, if you break No Contact or see something on social media, it doesn't mean you're back to square one. It just means you might have a few off days, but they will pass, and you'll keep making progress.

Normal Setbacks During Heartbreak

There are so many things that can make you feel like you've had a setback in getting over your ex. Some of these may be in your control, but a lot of them aren't. Following is a list of common setbacks you may have experienced. Check off any that you've been through and write down how long the impact was. What you'll realize is that these setbacks don't last long.

☐ Seeing your ex's social media

How long was the impact?

_____

_____

☐ Hearing about your ex from a mutual friend

How long was the impact?

_____

_____

☐ Seeing a friend get engaged

How long was the impact?

_____

_____

☐ Your ex's birthday

How long was the impact?

_____

_____

☐ Your anniversary

How long was the impact?

_____

_____

☐ Valentine's Day or any holiday

How long was the impact?

_____

_____

☐ Getting frustrated on dating apps

How long was the impact?

_____

_____

☐ Hearing from your ex's family member

How long was the impact?

_____

_____

☐ Going on a not-so-great date

How long was the impact?

_____

_____

☐ Going through something tough and wanting to reach out to your ex

How long was the impact?

_____

_____

☐ Actually seeing or talking to your ex

How long was the impact?

_____

_____

☐ Being really triggered by a memory of your ex

How long was the impact?

_____

_____

☐ Finding out your ex is seeing someone new

How long was the impact?

_____

_____

Setback Tool Kit

A setback may catapult you into feeling like the breakup just happened all over again. While setbacks do not mean you're back at the beginning, it's important to take extra-good care of yourself for the next few days. This might mean reaching out to people for support, practicing self-care, treating yourself, calling up your therapist, and anything else that will make you feel supported.

In the space provided, write down five things you can do for yourself if you go through a setback.

_____

_____

_____

_____

_____

It's also easy to feel frustrated or angry when you hit a setback, when what you really need is a lot of self-kindness and self-compassion. Write yourself a quick pep talk that you can read in the future when you're feeling down.

_____

_____

_____

_____

Planning Ahead

The best way to prevent setbacks is to be prepared. The reason it's so important to remove your ex on social media is so you don't accidentally see something about them that will cause a setback. It's also a good idea to tell your friends not to share information about your ex, so you can avoid hearing things about them that will trigger you.

Triggers can also come in the form of special occasions, such as a birthday (most people struggle on their birthdays and their exes' birthdays) or a friend's wedding. In this exercise, you'll write down any future potential setback triggers and how you're going to minimize them as much as possible. For example, if you're going to a friend's wedding soon, make sure you tell a friend who is also going to the wedding that you know it's going to be a hard day for you so they can make sure to be supportive of you at the wedding.

Write down any setback triggers that may be coming up in the future and how you will face them.

_____

_____

_____

_____

_____

_____

PART 3

HEALING AND REBUILDING Review

In this part, we dug deeper into your feelings around the breakup. You made great progress doing some self-reflection in order to build yourself back up again. This is where the long-lasting healing comes—when you can accept the breakup, accept your feelings, and process all of your emotions so you can move forward with a clean slate.

Let's Recap

Use these questions to recap this part before moving on to the next one.

✦

We talked about the importance of accepting the breakup for what it is. Even if you don't like the situation, even if you don't approve of how the relationship ended, it's vital to accept it so you can move on.

After completing the exercises in this part, is there anywhere you're still feeling stuck in your healing?

_____

_____

_____

_____

_____

_____

✦

We talked about how important it is to have a healthy outlet for anger and resentment, so these things don't come out sideways later on.

How did it feel to get your anger down on paper?

_____

_____

_____

_____

_____

_____

✦

As you continue to move forward in your healing, building your self-esteem and self-worth is crucial, especially if you have relied on romantic partners for your self-esteem and self-worth in the past.

After going through the exercises, what are some new behaviors you'll take with you to continue to empower yourself?

_____

_____

_____

_____

_____

_____

✦

We explored how living your life single is actually an incredible opportunity to reclaim parts of your life you may have lost during the relationship and foster new parts of yourself.

What are you looking forward to exploring in your single life?

_____

_____

_____

_____

_____

_____

PART
4

MOVING ON
IN YOUR
JOURNEY

You have reached the final part of the workbook! In this section, we will talk about how to start moving on from this breakup so you can explore dating and new relationships. At this point in your recovery, you may have already started dating again, which is great! You may also be panicking reading this part because you're nowhere close to even thinking about dating—that's okay too. You're moving at whatever pace is right for you.

This part of the workbook is going to serve as a helpful tool as you begin to fully close the door on your former relationship. While dating again is important, these exercises won't be about learning how to reply to someone on a dating app, how to set up your dating profile to seem the most attractive, or anything of that sort. As in the rest of this book, the focus will be on YOU and how you can move into the next phase of your life feeling confident, prepared, and excited while also honoring the fact that you're coming out of a heartbreak.

Before we move on, let's set the stage by discussing how you may be feeling about your breakup at the moment.

You may still have moments when you feel really heartbroken and stuck on your ex. The thought of dating might make you feel sick, and you may feel convinced that you'll never be able to find someone remotely as amazing as your ex. These feelings probably mean you just need some more time to heal and allow the work you're doing to set in. But feeling this way doesn't mean you're "doomed" or failing. You are going to get over your ex, and these feelings are going to pass.

On the other hand, you may be excited at the thought of dating, but anytime you look at someone new, all you're doing is comparing them to your ex. When you're on dating apps or just looking around in your day-to-day life, you can't help but think about your ex and how this new person you're looking at doesn't add up in some way. This behavior is also completely normal! Your brain loves to draw comparisons when it's approaching new territory, and especially if you were with your ex for a substantial amount of time, it makes sense that you're viewing new people in this way. This doesn't mean you're not over your ex yet or not ready to date—it just means you're a human being.

Or you may be ready to date but actually feel guilty about moving on. Surprise—this is also completely normal! It's incredibly common to feel like you're cheating on your ex when you go on a date or when you kiss someone new. This feeling comes from your brain getting used to you no longer being with your ex. You're not doing anything wrong; it's just another feeling that will pass.

Finally, it's normal to leave your first date in tears because you miss your ex. It can feel very discouraging, but don't let it derail your amazing progress so far. People often ask, "Do I need to be completely over my ex before I start dating again?" The answer is NO. Contrary to popular opinion, it isn't necessary to be completely over your ex before you start dating, and in reality, it's an advantage to start exploring dating before you are fully ready.

Why? Because all the healing work you're doing is very individual, and it can feel difficult to assess your progress if you don't try moving on. You're working hard via this workbook, your friends, and potentially a therapist, but you aren't necessarily putting your healing to the test. Trying out the dating apps or going out on dates will show you areas where you haven't yet fully healed. It's essentially a helpful spotlight on things you may not realize you haven't addressed. This doesn't mean you are doing anything wrong; it just means dating is unlocking a new level of growth and healing opportunities.

While it's not a good idea to start dating too soon, if you're feeling hesitant because you want to be certain you're over your ex, I will challenge you to try a date. The beauty is that you can try a couple of dates, and if you're not ready, you can go back to enjoying your life single! Just because you start doesn't mean you have to continue.

This final part of the workbook should also give you the boost of confidence you need to get back out into the dating world with optimism and joy. We will be going over three main themes in this part:

1. **How to leverage the opportunity of this breakup to make changes to how you date in the future.** Even though breakups are painful, they are a tremendous opportunity to pause and reflect on not just this last relationship but your previous relationships as well. By taking the time to go through lessons learned, you will have more clarity moving forward.

2. **How to move forward with confidence and assurance.** While it's normal to have fear and negative thoughts when you think about dating, it is important to have different tools to combat these thoughts so you don't end up in a self-fulfilling prophecy. If you believe that there is no one out there as good as your ex, your brain will confirm that for you. We will go through some ways to shift your mindset so you know

to your core that you always have another chance at love, it's never too late to find love, and there is an incredible partner out there waiting for you (very likely to be even better than your ex).

3. **How to get excited about your future!** Even though dating can be scary, it's also an exciting time when you get to meet new people and have fun. You will have the chance to visualize exactly what you want in a partner and define exactly how you want to feel. Taking the time to do these exercises will ensure that you don't jump into a relationship out of convenience or scarcity but rather find one that is fulfilling and satisfying to you.

Before you head off to the final exercises, don't forget to celebrate all the progress you've made so far in this workbook. Some of the things you did within this book weren't easy, but you made a huge investment in yourself. After finishing, don't be alarmed if thoughts about your ex come into your mind or if you have some hard days. That doesn't mean your healing didn't work; healing from heartbreak just takes time, and your path isn't always a straight line forward.

You can always come back to this workbook whenever you need to and redo the exercises or reread some of the things you wrote down. It can also be worthwhile to read what you wrote early on and see how far you have come. Always remember that you are stronger than you think, every broken heart will heal, and this too shall pass!

Hindsight Is 20/20

When you first go through a breakup, you mainly focus on the things that you lost. This means you're probably only looking at the good parts of your relationship and you're not able to see its faults. Of course, this makes the breakup feel worse, because it feels like you're losing a five-star relationship.

As you've gotten some distance from the relationship, you've been able to start seeing it more clearly. If someone had asked you right after the breakup to make a list of things you didn't like about your ex, you probably wouldn't have been able to think of much, but as time has passed, that list has likely gotten a little longer. This doesn't mean that your thoughts about your ex have changed; it just means that you're now more objective.

The reason it's important to think of what didn't work in your relationship is that you'll be able to see why it was actually a good thing it didn't work out. If you were meant to be with your ex, you would be with your ex. So by doing this reflecting, you'll start getting glimpses into why it didn't work out.

This reflection also doesn't mean you need to label your relationship as "bad"—you were with your ex for a reason. You'll just be able to feel at peace with the relationship ending, because you can confidently say it was for the best.

How Clear Is Your Hindsight?

Following is a list of true-or-false questions to determine whether you are able to see your ex and your relationship objectively at this point. If you're not at that place yet, don't worry! It might just take more time. If you still have your ex on a pedestal and/or you desperately want the relationship back, hang in there. Those feelings will pass.

I am able to see both the good and the bad parts of my last relationship.

True   False

I don't have my ex up on a pedestal; I can see their faults.

True   False

I believe that my relationship ended for a reason.

True   False

I believe my breakup was a blessing in disguise.

True   False

The way I see my relationship has changed since the breakup first happened.

True   False

If you answered "True" to most of these questions, it's likely that you've taken the time to objectively assess your relationship and breakup.

Ex on a Pedestal

One of the biggest obstacles to getting over a breakup is the inability to see your ex's negative qualities in addition to their positive ones. No partner should ever be up on a pedestal, because no one is perfect. By only seeing the good, you're making it seem as if you lost the "perfect" partner.

In this exercise, you're going to make an "ick" list of things about your ex that weren't a good match for you. This is not meant to bash your ex; it's just a way for you to see that your ex is a human being with faults and annoying qualities like anyone else. Don't worry about how many things you come up with—you can write down little things, like how they pronounced a certain word, to big things, like how they didn't like spending time with your family.

Write down your ex's "ick" list here.

How Have Your Views Changed?

Right after the breakup, you may not have been able to come up with a single thing you didn't like about your ex, you may have seen the relationship as perfect, or you may have been blindsided with no clues that the relationship was ending. Now that you have distance and time to become objective, your views about your ex, the relationship, or the actual breakup have likely changed. For example, if you were blindsided by the breakup at first, now you may be able to see the signs that the relationship was coming to a close.

Take some time to journal your thoughts on how your views of the relationship have changed since the breakup first happened.

_____

_____

_____

_____

_____

_____

_____

_____

_____

_____

Letter to Your Past Self

Think back to the version of yourself right after the breakup happened—the version of you who was curled up on the floor sobbing or felt like you couldn't make it through the day. Now that time has passed and you've done a lot of healing, what would you say to the past version of you?

Write a letter to yourself that you wish you could have read right after your breakup happened.

_____

_____

_____

_____

_____

_____

_____

_____

_____

_____

_____

_____

Discovering Patterns in Your Relationships

Going through a breakup is an opportunity to not just reflect on this last relationship that ended but also to think about your relationship history. You might find yourself feeling déjà vu, because it seems like you've been in this exact same situation before. Do you keep dating the same type of person? Do your breakups happen at the same point in the relationship or because of the same issue?

When you don't take the time after a relationship ends to reflect and process what just happened, it's easy to fall into patterns in your relationships, such as:

* Dating people who need to be "saved," whether that's financially, from mental health issues, or from low motivation
* Dating people who you think you can change
* Being with emotionally unavailable partners
* Going after people who you think are out of your league
* Dating people with a certain job or appearance

Almost everyone will fall into some kind of a pattern, and as you'll learn in the following exercises, the patterns aren't always bad. It's important to assess and be aware of the patterns you fall into, because you can't change or fix something you aren't aware of. In these next exercises, you'll look at your relationship patterns and how to start breaking any unhelpful habits as you move forward.

What Are Your Patterns?

One of your patterns could be how you have acted in relationships—for example, you tend to make yourself small and lose a part of yourself in the relationship. Another pattern could be how the relationships have played out—for example, they're hot and heavy in the beginning and then one person loses interest. Yet another pattern could be the type of person you find yourself in a relationship with—for example, someone who doesn't like to hang out with your friends. Look back on your last few relationships and dating experiences and look for similarities.

Can you recognize any negative patterns in your previous relationships?

_____

_____

_____

_____

_____

_____

_____

_____

_____

Just My Type

When talking to friends about dating and relationships, a common question is, "What's your type?" This can refer to physical, emotional, and/or character traits. It's a good idea to take some time to list what your type is so you are aware of what you're looking for and can assess whether dating someone that fits these criteria is the best plan for you. Your type may not have been totally consistent throughout your past relationships, but you might find some common threads. Take a few minutes to write your thoughts on these prompts.

What is your type?

_____

_____

_____

How has this type served you well?

_____

_____

_____

How has this type negatively affected you?

_____

_____

_____

Breaking the Habit

Now that you've identified some negative patterns, it's time to break those habits as you think about dating again. Sometimes just being aware that something is a pattern is enough to break it, but other times it takes a little more work.

Take, for example, if falling for emotionally unavailable partners is a pattern for you. You can tell yourself not to do that again, but what you really need to do is address the core issue. Typically, if you're falling for emotionally unavailable partners, it's because you don't feel worthy of being with someone who is available to you.

Do some journaling on what the core issues of your patterns might be. Once you think you've identified them, list some ways you can invest in yourself to break those patterns.

_____

_____

_____

_____

_____

_____

_____

_____

Holding On to Positive Patterns

Not all patterns are bad. In your experience in relationships, you've likely picked up some great habits and patterns, and those are the ones that you want to take with you into dating. You don't want to start completely from scratch—you can take these positive habits and patterns you've acquired and build upon them.

What are some of the behaviors, patterns, and/or attitudes you brought into your last few relationships that positively contributed to the relationships?

_____

_____

_____

_____

What are some of the behaviors, patterns, and/or attitudes that your previous partners had that positively contributed to the relationships?

_____

_____

_____

_____

_____

Finding Forgiveness

Forgiveness is an important part of the breakup-healing process. But it can feel almost impossible to forgive someone who broke your heart into a million pieces. In fact, sometimes being mad at your ex feels like the fuel you need to get over them—so why should you forgive them?

Holding on to anger and resentments causes so much stress on your mental and even your physical health. It can interfere with your future relationships and affect your ability to get close to or trust other people in the future. Being angry at your ex is also giving your ex the "upper hand" by keeping them in your thoughts. Healing from a breakup means not giving your ex your energy anymore, and holding on to anger prevents that.

There are a couple of misconceptions around forgiveness that prevent people from doing it. First, you may believe by forgiving your ex, you're letting them "get away with" something. You may also think that forgiving them means you're not standing up for yourself. Forgiving does not mean that you approve of someone's actions; it just means you're no longer willing to bear the burden of resentment.

The second misconception is that you have to forgive someone all at once for everything. Forgiveness can happen in stages—you can forgive one issue at a time. Some things might take longer to let go of, and that's okay. The more you forgive in bite-sized pieces, the more likely you are to eventually forgive entirely.

Write a Forgiveness Letter to Your Ex

It's time to write a letter to your ex forgiving them for whatever you're capable of forgiving at this time. This is NOT a letter that you'll send to your ex—this is just for you. If you don't feel ready to forgive certain hurtful or annoying things, don't include them in the letter. This is a process that might take some time.

Dear ex,

_____

_____

_____

_____

_____

_____

_____

_____

_____

_____

_____

Write a Forgiveness Letter to Yourself

Now it's time to write yourself a letter forgiving yourself for whatever you can at this time. If you're having trouble writing it, pretend you're offering forgiveness to a best friend and see if that mindset helps. Once you're done, read this letter out loud to yourself.

Dear self,

_____

_____

_____

_____

_____

_____

_____

_____

_____

_____

_____

_____

_____

Signs You're over Your Ex

As you continue to progress through your postbreakup healing, you'll start wondering when you're going to be completely over your ex. You might imagine that once you hit this finish line, you'll no longer have to think about them. Unfortunately (and fortunately), that's not how it works. There isn't some theatrical moment that signifies you're over your breakup; it's much more subtle than that.

Just like healing, feeling "over" your breakup is a continuous process of releasing your connections to the relationship little by little. Every time you let go of one of these connections, the weight on your heart will feel lighter. Then one day it will hit you that you feel okay and you've felt okay for many days in a row.

The signs of being over an ex look different for everyone. For some it means being able to see them out in public and not be affected by it. For others it means hearing that they're dating someone new and being okay with it. Others might know they're over their ex when they genuinely hope the best for them. If these goals sound too lofty, that's okay too. These things take time, and remember—every small win means you're getting closer to getting over your ex.

Instead of looking at a finish line far off in the distance, the best course of action is to look back at how far you've come.

Where You Came From

Think back to the hours and days following your breakup. It probably felt like the pain would never go away, and you couldn't fathom how you were going to work the next day. When you look back on how you felt then versus now, you're going to feel proud of how much progress you've made.

In the space here, journal on the differences from the beginning to now. Did you go from curled up in a ball on your floor to being able to function on a day-to-day basis? Did you constantly wait for your ex to call, but now you can go a day without thinking about them? Track your journey here.

_____

_____

_____

_____

_____

_____

_____

_____

_____

_____

Small Wins

Getting over a breakup is incredibly tough, so you should acknowledge and celebrate every small win you achieve. In the previous exercise, you journaled about the emotional progress you've made since the breakup first happened. Here you're going to list all the little victories you've had.

Examples include going to the restaurant where you had your first date with your ex, not texting your ex on a birthday or other special occasion, going out to dinner on your own, booking a trip you've always wanted to go on, signing up for a dating app, being able to delete your ex from social media, replacing the photos around your house with photos of your friends instead, or anything else you've accomplished, no matter how small it may seem.

Write down a list of the small victories you've had on your journey to get over your ex.

_____

_____

_____

_____

_____

_____

_____

Visualize Being Completely over Your Ex

Being completely over a breakup is going to be different for everyone, but it's important to know what being over a breakup feels and looks like to *you*. This exercise gives you time to consider that.

Take 5–10 minutes to visualize what it will feel like when you're over your ex. Write down what you imagine in as detailed a way as possible. How will it feel emotionally? How will you act differently?

_____

_____

_____

_____

_____

_____

_____

_____

_____

_____

_____

Are You over Your Ex? A Checklist

Following is a checklist of signs you're over your ex or, more importantly, in the process of getting over your ex. This is a checklist of common signs—but remember, this is a personal journey, so if you haven't experienced these, don't worry. Everyone moves at their own pace.

Check off any of these that apply to you:

☐ Being excited about dating again

☐ Being able to listen to music that reminds you of your ex

☐ Not wanting to contact your ex

☐ Not thinking it's your ex every time your phone rings

☐ Being able to talk about the breakup without getting emotional

☐ Seeing your relationship objectively

☐ Not thinking about your ex obsessively anymore

☐ Finding out your ex is dating someone else and not being upset

☐ Being able to look at old photos and just see them as good memories

☐ Not wanting to look at your ex's social media

☐ Knowing that your ex wasn't "the one" and being okay with it

☐ Significant dates passing and you feeling okay

☐ Enjoying your time single

- ☐ Going days without thinking about your ex
- ☐ Going days and then weeks without crying
- ☐ Running into your ex and not feeling overwhelmed
- ☐ No longer hoping you and your ex will get back together
- ☐ Seeing your ex as just another person, not a perfect person and not a horrible person
- ☐ Forgiving your ex
- ☐ Feeling at peace when thinking about the breakup
- ☐ Genuinely wishing your ex the best
- ☐ No longer dreaming about your ex
- ☐ Memories evoking appreciation and not hurt
- ☐ Your ex not being your first thought when you wake up
- ☐ No longer plotting ways to run into your ex
- ☐ No longer obsessing about what your ex is doing

Lessons Learned

Dating and being in relationships is how you learn what you like and don't like in a partner. It's also how you learn how to act and how you want to feel when you're in a relationship. This is why no relationship is a waste of time—each one will teach you either what you want or what you don't want.

Many people don't take the time to pause and reflect after a relationship to figure out what went well and what didn't go well. When you don't reflect, you may either end up dating the exact same type of person again or going to the complete opposite, neither of which will serve you.

Not only do relationships have so many lessons within them, but so does the actual process of the breakup. When you're put into an extremely stressful situation, it's an opportunity to learn about yourself and how you operate. Pain is a huge motivator, and many people take the opportunity of a breakup to start going to therapy, which may lead to them digging into issues that are not even related to the breakup.

All these lessons lead you forward, toward a happy future. The exercises in this section will help you make sure you don't miss any lessons along the way.

Learning about You

It's time to think about what you've learned from this breakup. It could be how you handle stress and pain, it could be about some past issues that you need to deal with, or it could be a realization that you need to be more independent. Then pivot to thinking about what surprised you about the process. Maybe you never thought you were someone who leaned on others, but you discovered you love getting others to help you. Or maybe you didn't think you were an emotional person, but once you gave yourself permission to feel, you found you are indeed a person who feels emotions deeply and you like that about yourself. There are no wrong answers here!

What has been the biggest thing you've learned about yourself through this breakup?

_____

_____

_____

_____

What has surprised you about yourself in the healing process?

_____

_____

_____

_____

Changing Habits

Learning about yourself and what you like and don't like in relationships can serve a very practical function once you start dating again. You can take the lessons you've learned and use them as a filter to weed out partners you've realized don't work well for you.

When you start dating again, how will you be wiser in selecting partners based on what you've learned from this breakup?

_____

_____

_____

_____

_____

_____

_____

_____

_____

_____

_____

_____

Blessings in Disguise

Blessings in disguise happen all the time. Maybe you get fired from a job only to find a much better job. Your bid on a house isn't accepted but then you find an amazing place the next week. Breakups are the ultimate examples of blessings in disguise, but the upsides usually take a while to show up. You may or may not yet believe that it's a good thing your breakup happened, but I can assure you, at some point in the future, you will.

If you're not at that place yet, there are still plenty of other opportunities to recognize blessings in disguise. It's important to acknowledge these, because the more you believe they happen, the more you'll notice when they occur in your life. If you have a hard time believing it, think back to past relationships that you thought were "the one." You can probably laugh about them now. In this activity, list blessings that you've noticed. They could include getting back into therapy, reconnecting with old friends, taking the trip you always wanted to, finding a new fitness class that you love, or discovering some new music. Get creative here!

List blessings in disguise that have happened since the breakup.

_____

_____

_____

_____

_____

Self-Assessment

In the "Could Have"s and "Should Have"s activity, we talked about how unproductive it is to second-guess yourself and think about scenarios that would have changed the breakup. It's true that no good will come out of trying to change the past. However, when you're able to be objective, it is productive to look back on how you acted in the relationship to see if there are any lessons you can learn.

In the nicest way possible, take some time to write down any changes you'd like to make personally now or once you start dating again. How do you want to act differently within your next relationship?

_____

_____

_____

_____

_____

_____

_____

_____

_____

_____

Are You Afraid of Getting Hurt Again?

Once you're finally seeing the light at the end of the tunnel of this breakup, a new fear sets in: the fear of getting hurt again. You survived this breakup, but you're not sure you can handle another one. You're starting to get curious about dating again, but this fear of potentially getting hurt again might stop you from doing that.

There is no guarantee that you'll never get hurt again in relationships unless you write off relationships completely (and who wants to do that?). But the trick is to do whatever you can to prevent yourself from getting hurt. Let's pretend you like to skateboard, and one day you have a bad fall and really hurt your knee. Are you going to give up skateboarding forever? Hopefully not. What can you do instead? Next time you go, you'll wear kneepads so you can protect your knee.

The same thing goes with relationships. Taking the time to do all this processing and reflecting on your past relationships sets you up for success and decreases the chances that you'll get hurt again. That said, it is completely normal to be nervous as you start dating. It's normal to cry after your first date, and it's normal to compare everyone to your ex. The following exercises will help you let go of the fear of getting hurt again, allow you to see that you *can* trust yourself, and help you get excited about this new chapter in your life!

Scarcity Mindset

Perhaps the most common fear-based thought after a breakup is, "I'm never going to find anyone ever again." Almost everyone going through a breakup has that thought at some point, but it's important to remind yourself again and again that it's not true.

You don't get a finite number of chances to find love. There is no age limit on finding love. Just because you're coming out of a good relationship doesn't mean you won't find an equally great, if not better, relationship. It's normal to have fears, but combat these thoughts so you can continue moving on.

Following are some common fear-based thoughts along with affirmations to help combat them. Read these affirmations as often as the thoughts come into your mind. You'll see space to write your own as well.

FEAR	AFFIRMATION
You only get one or two good relationships in your lifetime.	I always have a chance to find a great relationship.
You will never find love.	I know a great relationship is coming my way.
Once you reach a certain age, you lose your chance at finding love.	It is never too late for me to find love.

FEAR	AFFIRMATION
Your ex was the best you were ever going to get.	➡ I can't wait to see what the future brings me.
You'll never get over your ex.	➡ My heartbreak will pass, and someday I'll see exactly why this breakup happened.

Survey: Are You Ready to Start Dating Again?

Let's assess where you are in terms of feeling ready to start dating again. Answer on a scale of 1–10 how much you agree with each statement; "1" means you don't agree at all and "10" means that you agree completely.

STATEMENT	RATING
I feel confident getting back into dating.	————
I trust that I will find another great relationship.	————
I am confident in my ability to choose good partners for myself.	————
I trust that even if the first person I go on a date with doesn't work out, I'm still going to be okay.	————
Even though I am ready to start dating again, I feel really confident in myself as a single person.	————
I trust that if someone isn't right for me, I will walk away.	————
I feel confident in my ability to spot red flags.	————
I trust that if my first few dates don't go well, it doesn't mean anything about how the rest of my dates will go.	————

Red Flags

When you're starting to date again, something you'll probably hear a lot is to "look out for red flags." Of course, you want to be aware of red flags, but you need to take the time to figure out what those are for you. Everyone is different, and something that may not be a problem for someone else could be a huge red flag for you. If you don't take the time to define your red flags in the beginning, you increase the chances that you'll ignore them as they come up.

Red flags can be external or internal. An internal red flag is something you notice about yourself in the relationship—for example, if you start ditching your friends to hang out with the person you're dating. That could be a red flag that you're diving into the relationship too fast. An external red flag is something in the other person—for example, if they don't believe in defining what a relationship is and quickly change the subject when you bring up your relationship.

In the space here, list red flags that you'll be on the lookout for, both in yourself and in others. When you're dating, keep referring to this list.

_____   _____

_____   _____

_____   _____

_____   _____

_____   _____

Your "Kneepads"

Remember that analogy of getting hurt while skateboarding? Getting hurt doesn't mean you stop skateboarding entirely; you just learn how to protect yourself better. In this exercise, you will write down your "kneepads"—things that will help prevent you from getting hurt in the future.

You're going to write down the specifics of how you were hurt in this relationship and breakup and then the kneepad you will use moving forward. For example, you might have found out that your ex was not ready for a committed relationship and that's why they broke up with you. Your kneepad might be clarifying within the first three months of dating that you are interested in a committed relationship.

Hurt: _____

Kneepad: _____

Hurt: _____

Kneepad: _____

Hurt: _____

Kneepad: _____

Knowing What You Want

When coming out of a breakup, it's important to be alert to both what you want to avoid in future relationships, and what you do want in a relationship. You may have a pretty good picture in your mind of what you want in a partner, but there is a lot of power in getting it down on paper.

Taking the time to figure out what you really want in a partner and in a relationship shows a strong commitment to yourself and will greatly increase your chances of getting what you want. When you start dating and find someone you connect with, you get hit with feel-good brain chemicals that can cloud your judgment. If you're not firm in what you want and don't want, those butterflies and flying sparks can land you in a relationship that's not right for you. You're also now equipped with so much more knowledge about yourself and your history in relationships, so you should feel confident making this list.

As you start laying out your dream partner and relationship, think back to the section on self-esteem and self-worth. If you start feeling like you're asking for "too much" or you're setting too high of a standard, remember that you are worthy of asking for what you want in a relationship.

That's why, in the following exercises, you won't just be asked to consider the attributes you want in a partner—physical features, characteristics, and values—you'll also be asked to describe how you want to feel in the relationship.

The Nonnegotiable Contract

There's a difference between nonnegotiables and red flags. Red flags are indicators that there *may* be some problematic behavior in the person. Nonnegotiables are full roadblocks that mean you abandon ship and walk the other way. Examples include not wanting to get married if that's something you want, not wanting to have kids if that's what you want, or being overly jealous or controlling.

This exercise will ask you to share your nonnegotiable contract with a friend for accountability. This is important, because having a friend who knows what you want and don't want will help you avoid a problematic partner.

Fill out a contract with yourself committing to the things you want or will avoid in future dating and relationships.

MY DATING PREFERENCES

My nonnegotiables are:

I'm committing to this because:

If I encounter this in the future, I will:

I have shared this with _____ for accountability.

Signed: _____

Build-a-Partner

This exercise is a brainstorming session to outline everything you desire in a future partner. It can include the big stuff, like their values and characteristics, but it can (and should) include the little things too—what movies they like to watch, what they do with their weekends, where they want to travel. This list isn't necessarily meant to be used as a checklist to determine whether a partner is a good fit—it's more for you to do a detailed visualization of what your future partner could be like.

Write down everything you want in a future partner.

_____

_____

_____

_____

_____

_____

_____

_____

_____

_____

How Do You Want to Feel in a Relationship?

When thinking about what you want in a future relationship, there is a lot of emphasis on what your partner looks like, what they do for a living, and what kind of characteristics they have. But that's missing a huge element: how they make you feel. When you're looking for a long-term, committed relationship, you need to consider how this person is going to make you feel. How are they going to make you feel safe? How will you feel when you see their name on your phone? How will it feel when they show you physical affection? Characteristics, physical features, and financial security are great, but how someone makes you feel indicates whether a relationship can thrive.

How do you want to feel when you're around this person?

_____

_____

_____

_____

How do you want your future partner to describe you?

_____

_____

_____

_____

What does it mean for you to feel safe in a relationship?

_____

_____

_____

_____

_____

_____

_____

How do you want to maintain the empowerment you've gained while being single as you go into this next relationship?

_____

_____

_____

_____

_____

_____

_____

_____

Grade Your Date

Once you start dating again, you can use this exercise to see if the person lines up with all the work you've been doing in this workbook.

Does this person go against any of my nonnegotiables?

_____

Does this person match up with most of my dream list?

_____

Does this person have any of the red flags that I've identified?

_____

How does this person make me feel?

_____

If I look back on everything I went through in my breakup and all the work I've done in this workbook, do I honestly feel like I should continue seeing this person?

_____

_____

_____

_____

Attract What You Promote

You hear the term "personal branding" all over social media. Your personal brand isn't just what you have on your *Instagram*; it's what you show others on a daily basis. Your personal brand is made up of how you dress, the energy you bring to a room, your communication style, your daily routine, what you like to do for fun, what you value, the people you surround yourself with, and more.

This overall message you put out to the world is likely how you attracted your group of friends and ended up in the career you have, and it is also how you bring potential partners into your sphere. The saying "You attract what you promote" is crucial when considering your upcoming dating journey.

To be clear, you deserve the partner you want, and you deserve to get all of your needs met. But it's worth considering what you're putting out there to be sure it matches who you want to bring in. For example, if you're someone who wants a partner who loves the outdoors, it's a good idea for you to be prioritizing time outdoors. On a more emotional level, if you want someone who is good at communicating their feelings, you need to make sure that you're communicating your feelings to those around you. Essentially, you can't ask something of someone that you won't do yourself. The following exercises will help you think about what you are showing the world and yourself to be sure it is in sync with what you want in a relationship.

Getting What You Want

In this exercise, you are going to pick the top ten things you want in a partner (you can use your list from the earlier Build-a-Partner exercise) and list them here. Then you will write down what actions you will take in order to attract that kind of person into your life. Here are a few examples:

✳ If you want a partner who likes to travel, plan a couple of weekend trips in the next few months.
✳ If you want a partner who is financially secure, go through your finances and make sure they're all in order.

Think about your values and hobbies as you write this list.

Use this space to write down ten things you want in a partner and how your behavior and actions can match that.

1 _____

_____

_____

2 _____

_____

_____

3 _____

_____

_____

4 _____

_____

_____

5 _____

_____

_____

6 _____

_____

_____

7 _____

_____

_____

8 _____

_____

_____

9 _____

_____

_____

10 _____

_____

_____

Where Can I Meet Someone?

As you start dating, you may wonder, "Where can I meet someone?" Online dating is a great option, but there are plenty of other ways to meet people too.

One technique for thinking of where to meet someone is to consider the kind of person you want to meet, then ask, "Where would this person be on a Saturday morning?" If you want someone who prioritizes hiking on the weekend, it's less likely that you'll find them at a bar late on a Friday night. If you want someone who loves to cook, you might want to start going to your local farmer's market. This obviously isn't an exact science, but it's focusing the energy you're putting out there. You're telling the world, "I know what I want, and I'm willing to try some new things to get it."

Think about the kind of partner you want and then write down some ideas of where that kind of person might be and when. What can you do to place yourself in similar situations?

_____

_____

_____

_____

_____

_____

_____

Refining Your List

When reflecting on the Attract What You Promote and Knowing What You Want sections, you may realize that some of the things you originally thought you wanted in a partner aren't that important to you at all. Unfortunately, social media will often tell you certain things should be important in your relationship when they really aren't important to you at all upon reflection.

For example, because of social media you might think you want a super-romantic partner who showers you with gifts and writes you sappy love notes. But as you go through these exercises, you may realize that you're not a particularly romantic person. That's okay! You don't have to be romantic and neither does your partner. It's okay to adjust your list as you look deeper into this concept.

Is there anything you want to change or take off your ideal-partner list as we come to the end of the Moving On in Your Journey part of this workbook?

_____

_____

_____

_____

_____

_____

_____

PART 4

MOVING ON IN YOUR JOURNEY *Review*

In this part, we went over everything you need in order to feel prepared and equipped to move on from this breakup and start dating again. It's normal to still have some fear about it, but because you now have a wealth of tools and techniques at your disposal, you can look ahead with confidence, excitement, and positive energy.

Let's Recap

Use these questions to recap this part.

✦

We went over how to fully utilize and embrace the lessons this last relationship and previous relationships have taught you. No relationship is a waste of time, and these exercises should prove that.

Do you feel like you have a good understanding of what lessons came out of your last relationship?

_____

_____

_____

_____

_____

_____

✦

We addressed the fear of getting hurt again, and while you can't guarantee you'll never get hurt in another relationship, you can be as prepared as possible (with your "kneepads").

Are you feeling more confident as you look to start dating again?

_____

_____

_____

_____

_____

_____

✦

Finally, we dived into getting a clear picture of what you want your future relationship to look like—not just your dream partner, but how you want to feel and act in a future relationship.

After going through the exercises, do you have a good grasp on what you want your future relationship and partner to be like?

_____

_____

_____

_____

_____

_____

INDEX